THE THEOLOGY OF ALBERT SCHWEITZER

THE WORKS OF ALBERT SCHWEITZER

✶

THE THEOLOGY OF
ALBERT SCHWEITZER
FOR CHRISTIAN INQUIRERS

BY

E. N. MOZLEY

WITH AN EPILOGUE BY
ALBERT SCHWEITZER

NEW YORK
THE MACMILLAN COMPANY
1951

Contents

Note

The references given at the end of passages quoted from Dr. Schweitzer's works are as follows:

Q. *The Quest of the Historical Jesus.* Translated by W. Montgomery. Second Edition.

M. *The Mystery of the Kingdom of God.* Translated by Walter Lowrie.

P. *Paul and his Interpreters.* Translated by W. Montgomery.

MP. *The Mysticism of Paul the Apostle.* Translated by W. Montgomery and F. C. Burkitt.

The following are among the principal sayings of Our Lord which relate to Dr. Schweitzer's teaching on New Testament eschatology:

St. Matthew X. 5 and (especially) 23.
St. Matthew XXV. 31.
St. Mark IV. 11–12.
St. Mark IX. 1.
St. Mark XIII. 24–30.
St. Mark XIV. 61–62.

Introduction

After studying the works of Albert Schweitzer I became profoundly impressed by his ideas concerning the life of Jesus and the teaching of the Apostle Paul. I therefore set out to give a short résumé of Dr. Schweitzer's theology and to offer it to those who are only vaguely aware of it, for I generally find almost entire ignorance about it, and as yet Schweitzer's teaching is not heard on the radio.

My part in this book lies mainly in the selection and arrangement of extracts from his theological works. But any value which this book may possess is immeasurably enhanced by the substantial Epilogue which Dr. Schweitzer has written for it and which (translated by J. R. Coates) forms the second part of the book. Despite his almost overwhelmingly busy life in Africa he set aside his first intention to write a short Introduction and made it the opportunity, forty years after the appearance of his *Quest of the Historical Jesus,* to develop more fully his thought concerning the effect upon Christian belief of non-fulfilment, and his views upon the significance of the idea of the Kingdom of God throughout history and at the present time. I feel both honoured and grateful to be able to include this masterly statement of his matured conclusions on the central problem of his religious thinking, and this message of deep importance to the world today.

Of Dr. Schweitzer himself, that supremely great and

good man, the Alsatian medical missionary who has been for over 30 years at Lambaréné in French Equatorial Africa, it has been asserted through a vote in a learned continental journal that, with Leonardo da Vinci and Goethe, Schweitzer completes the greatest trio of intellectual "all-rounders" that can be found in the Christian Era. Within the spheres of art and of thought that place for Schweitzer can hardly be denied. A graduate of Strasbourg University who before he was thirty was a Doctor of Theology, a Doctor of Philosophy and a Doctor of Music and in the front rank throughout Europe in all three, he, at that age, proceeded by seven years of service, like Jacob, to earn his doctorate of medicine. Today he stands in the front rank in experience and practice of tropical medicine. With his own hands he contributed largely to the building of his hospitals on the Equator. This man needs no advertisement to the world. He is indeed almost a *lusus naturæ*. But Dr. Schweitzer, as all the world knows that knows about these things, is far greater even than these spiritual activities show forth. He is a human being who from his 'twenties' planned his life as an offering to God solely and fully in the service of his fellow-creatures, dedicating his powers and his life that he might repay to the people of Africa the tremendous and dreadful debt amassed through centuries of cruelty by that other continent, Europe.

Schweitzer has written in the main four great religious works. In 1901 (1905 in English) was published *The Mystery of the Kingdom of God*. In 1906 (1910 in English) there followed *The Quest of the Historical Jesus*. The first 340 of the 400 pages of *The Quest*, which is his most famous theological work, is devoted to the history of German theology, as

2

its original title "From Reimarus to Wrede" showed. In other respects these two volumes cover the same ground, the eschatological thought, teaching and consequent life of Jesus. His other two great works deal with St. Paul, *Paul and His Interpreters*, and *The Mysticism of Paul the Apostle*. These also are concerned mainly with eschatology, that of St. Paul. Dr. Schweitzer has also written a smaller but most interesting book about Oriental religious thought. *Christianity and the Religions of the World*. Nor must the student of his theology omit to read Chapter VI and also the Epilogue of his autobiography *My Life and Thought* where his religious thought is set forth with especial clearness.

The present work is an endeavour to comprise in a very small volume the essentials of the theological thought of Schweitzer. I have here collected from these four volumes in what seemed to be the best sequence the main heads of his thought concerning the eschatology of Jesus and His followers.

In this introduction it is not unfitting to clear the ground somewhat. Schweitzer's exposition may alarm the reader, brought up in conventional theology, by indicating what Jesus did *not* believe, what matters were *not* those next to his heart and what, therefore, he did *not* teach.

As will be obvious, if Jesus expected an almost immediate end to this earth as man's home, normal ethical and social progress hardly appears in the words of Jesus or in His thought: he will not teach us a "slow perfection of the world." Nor, according to Schweitzer, did the religion of Jesus consist (as represented in much modern thought) mainly in the stressing of the fatherhood of God and the brotherhood of man. Schweitzer speaks of such as a narrow

3

and peculiarly insipid conception of His religion. "Jesus is an authority for us, not in the sphere of knowledge, but only in the matter of the will."

The reader should learn further of the following important view advanced by Schweitzer. It is found in a footnote on page 233 of *The Mysticism of Paul the Apostle* relevant to the apparent fact that Jesus gave but one command to baptise:

"That tradition putting the commandment to baptize into the mouth of Jesus *after* His resurrection (Matthew xxviii. 19-20) shows that we have here to do with a later view. And this is confirmed by the fact that the baptismal command pre-supposes not baptism in the name of Christ, but of Father, Son and Spirit."

So much for the negative side. Turning to the basis of the eschatological teaching of Jesus, we are first reminded that He built it largely on Deutero-Isaiah, on the minor prophets and on the apocalyptic books, Daniel, and the Similitudes of Enoch, and we are told of the likeness of His thought to much that is found in the Apocalypses of Baruch and Ezra.

In the body of the present book will be found Dr. Schweitzer's explanation of the relevant texts, mainly in the Synoptic Gospels, but also in the Fourth Gospel and in St. Paul (principally in Thessalonians I). Schweitzer also describes the attitude of the Church, immediately after the Crucifixion, and the general fading away of Christian eschatological expectation as the years passed on and yet the parousia (reappearance) of Jesus never took place.

"The true continuation of the Gospel of Jesus is found only in the authentic Primitive-Christian eschatological Paulinism. This alone is the Gospel of Jesus in the form ap-

4

propriate to the time subsequent to His death." (MP. 392.)

"Had Paulinism been a Hellenized Christianity it would have been influential as such in the immediately following period. The fact that even the second generation does not know what to make of his teaching, suggests the conjecture that he built his system upon a conviction which ruled only in the first generation. But what was it that disappeared out of the first Christian generation? What but the expectation of the immediate dawn of the Messianic Kingdom of Jesus?" (MP. 39).

"Ignatius, in his Epistle to the Ephesians (about A.D. 110), holds that 'the last times have come.' The Apocalypse of John closed with the words, 'surely I come quickly. Amen. Come, Lord Jesus!' (Revelation xxii. 20). In the Epistle of Barnabas, doubtless to be dated about the end of the first century, we read: 'Near is the day on which for the wicked all is lost; near is the Lord and His reward.'" (MP. 336).

"For Polycarp, the Bishop of Smyrna, who wrote about the same time to the Philippians, the resurrection still signifies being associated with Christ in ruling in the Messianic Kingdom." (MP. 336–7.)

"What a strong hold the eschatological expectation still had in the Church in Asia Minor about the middle of the second century A.D. is shown by the rise of Montanism. This enthusiastic movement, which began in Mysia was determined to give to the belief in the immediate nearness of the Kingdom the same importance as it had in Primitive Christianity.

"That the delay of the return of the Lord awakened doubts as to the certainty of the Coming of the Messianic Kingdom we know from some of the New Testament Epistles. The

5

writer of the Epistle to the Hebrews is obliged to exhort believers not to give up hope, but to remain steadfast to the end." (Hebrews vi. 11–12, x. 23, 35, xii. 12–14). (MP. 337).

"The Second Epistle of Peter points out, as against the mockers who asserted that the return of Christ would not take place at all, that God's reckoning of time is not like man's, for a thousand years are in His sight as a single day. If he still delayed the Coming of Christ it was from long-suffering, to give men further time for repentance (2 Peter iii. 4–9).

"According to the Epistle of Jude the attitude of the scorners in regard to the delay of redemption is the sign that it is near at hand, since, according to the words of the Apostles, there should come in the last time mockers (Jude 17–23).

"Justin, too, has to admit that not all believers still live in the expectation of the New Jerusalem. Justin writes:—'But that, on the other hand, even among Christians of a pure and pious temper, many do not share this view I have already indicated.'

"In general, therefore, it must be concluded, up to near the middle of the second century, at least in the Church in Asia Minor, of which we know something from Ignatius, Polycarp, and Papias, the eschatological hope still formed a living element in Christian belief." (MP. 337–8).

"From the moment when believers have no longer the consciousness of being the single generation 'upon which the End of the Times has come' (I Corinthians x. 11), and which alone is to share in the Messianic Kingdom, the intensification of the eschatological expectation into the escha-

6

tological mysticism of the dying and rising with Christ is no longer possible." (MP. 339).

Of the Fourth Gospel Dr. Schweitzer writes:

"How much living eschatological expectation the Johannine Gospel still presupposes is hard to make out. Certainly a visible Coming of the Son of Man and a general resurrection for judgment are expected.

"John v. 26–27: 'For as the Father has life in Himself, so also has He given to the Son to have life in Himself. And He has given Him authority to hold a judgment also, because He is the Son of Man. Wonder not at this, for the hour is coming at which all those who are in the graves shall hear His voice, and shall come forth, those that have done good to the resurrection of life, those that have done evil to the resurrection of judgment.'" (MP. 368.)

The following passage gives a clear picture of what the eschatology held and taught by Jesus means to Dr. Schweitzer:

"The primary and all-controlling fact of the religious experience of Jesus was his God-consciousness—his consciousness of God as Father. Nothing is more obvious than that out of that consciousness he acted and spoke *immediately*. And when his acts were influenced and his speech coloured by the eschatological outlook, what was that ultimately but the consciousness of God's *nearness*? How could the expectation of a divine world be so constant and so vivid without the feeling that it is in a sense locally near, imminent, impending, ready to break in, indeed actually intruding upon this present world, as it were 'the finger of God' touching us here? Intuitional feeling, presentiment, insight, do not readily distinguish between nearness in time and in space.

7

Jesus' eschatology was an expression of his God-conscious-ness—the most eminent expression of it."

And again,

"The most fundamentally important religious exercise is the practice of the presence of God." (M. 40 and 43.)

Finally, thus does this devoted follower of Jesus speak of his Master:

"And yet in all His speech and action the Messianic con-sciousness shines forth. One might, indeed, speak of the acts of His Messianic consciousness. The Beatitudes, nay, the whole of the Sermon on the Mount, with the authoritative 'I' for ever breaking through, bear witness to the high dignity which He ascribed to Himself. Did not this 'I' set the people thinking?" (Q. 370.)

As the compiler of this little book I am but a humble in-troducer of the reader to Albert Schweitzer and through him to what Schweitzer believes to be the true thought about Jesus. It is perhaps not unnatural that, as a great-nephew of a Regius Professor of Divinity at Oxford and (on another side of my family) of Cardinal Newman, I should have given much thought to theological questions. But most of the text which follows is built, as assuredly the reader would have it, upon the printed words of the master of Strasbourg and of Lambaréné.

E. N. MOZLEY
D.S.O., LT. COL., R.E. (RET.)

1949

1. The Original Reception of the Theological Works of Dr. Schweitzer

Perhaps the most vivid description of the effect upon the world of theological thought produced by the publications in English of *The Mystery of the Kingdom of God* in 1905, and (still more) of *The Quest of the Historical Jesus* in 1910, is that which was given to the writer by Dr. Micklem, Principal of Mansfield College, Oxford. He said, "The publication of Dr. Schweitzer's book (*The Quest*) was like the explosion of a vast bomb in the theological world. It finally blew up the nineteenth century liberalistic interpretation of the life and teaching of our Lord."

In Germany it was seen that a result of Schweitzer's exposition had been an attack on the 'Liberal' Life of Jesus, so his book met with passive hostility there. But Britain was more friendly. The greatest interest was at once shown, and Professor Sanday enthusiastically accepted Schweitzer's position (though Sanday withdrew somewhat in 1907 perhaps under the influence of scholarly timidity). In America but little interest was at first taken in Dr. Schweitzer.

One has to look far in British theological expositions today to find Schweitzer's teaching investigated and explained in publications, or made known in addresses and sermons, or broadcast to the lay public. This has been more than unfortunate; it has been unfair to the general Christian world, which is always entitled to know what the best contemporary Christian writers are saying.

In happy contrast to this somewhat mediæval policy of silence and restriction it may be proper to quote the first words of the preface of the English translation of *The Quest* by one of the most learned of our theologians, the late Dr. Burkitt, one-time Norris-Hulse Professor of theology at Cambridge:

"The book here translated is offered to the English-speaking public in the belief that it sets before them, as no other book has ever done, the history of the struggle which the best-equipped intellects of the modern world have gone through in endeavouring to realise for themselves the historical personality of our Lord.

"Everyone nowadays is aware that traditional Christian doctrine about Jesus Christ is encompassed with difficulties, and that many of the statements in the Gospels appear incredible in the light of modern views of history and nature." (Q.V.)

It is lastly appropriate to bring to the notice of the reader Dr. Schweitzer's first four lines of *The Quest* itself:

"When, at some future day, our period of civilization shall lie, closed and completed, before the eyes of later generations, German theology will stand out as a great, a unique phenomenon in the mental and spiritual life of our time." (Q. 1.) We shall then come to know our debt to a great country.

2. The "Liberal-minded" Jesus as portrayed by modern conventional theology

"The Jesus of Nazareth who appeared as the Messiah, proclaimed the morality of the kingdom of God, established the kingdom of heaven upon earth, and died in order to consecrate his work—this Jesus never existed. It is a figure sketched by Rationalism, enlivened by Liberalism, and dressed up by modern theology in the clothes of historical science." (M. 26.)

". . . . . the Jesus of modern theology is so extraordinarily lifeless. Left in his eschatological world he is greater and, for all the strangeness, he affects us more elementally, more mightily than the modern Jesus." (M. 49.)

"Conservative theology, like the older orthodoxy to which it is akin, was not able to do anything with the historical Jesus, because it likewise makes far too little of the great moral ideas which in his eschatology were struggling for life and practical expression." (M. 52.)

". . . . . modern theology does violence to history and psychology, inasmuch as it cannot prove what right we have to segregate Jesus from his age, to translate his personality into the terms of our modern thought, and to conceive of him as 'Messiah' and 'Son of God' outside of the Jewish framework." (M. 250–1.)

Passages such as these shew clearly the broad trend of Dr. Albert Schweitzer's Christology. Finally on the last page of *The Quest*, Schweitzer writes:

". . . it is a good thing that the true historical Jesus should overthrow the modern Jesus, should rise up against the modern spirit and send upon earth, not peace, but a sword.

11

He was not teacher, not a casuist; He was an imperious ruler. It was because He was so in His inmost being that He could — think of Himself as the Son of Man." (Q. 401.)

It is with words such as these that Dr. Schweitzer opens fire upon conventional Christian theology. He claims and subsequently demonstrates how deeply Christians have been misled, almost from the apostolic age. This misleading has only been possible through unthinking piety, and in the middle ages through more sinister methods, a mingling of sacerdotal assertion and, only too often of cruelties, among which the Inquisition darkly looms. Just as the age-long servile obedience of the German people has brought upon them and upon us the horrors of totalitarian dominance, so has clerical dominance, even after the Reformation, forbidden the exposition of free theological thought and has brought about widespread and deep ignorance.

Those who diligently read the first 349 pages of *The Quest* will learn how certain learned and courageous German theologians since the 18th century (together with some French and British help) forged their way to theological freedom and finally towards Dr. Schweitzer's position. But of all this the Christian people of our country have been told but little by their own Christian ministers.

And with the following passages in the last chapter of *The Quest* Dr. Schweitzer makes plain the vital errors of conventional Christian thought.

"The study of the Life of Jesus has had a curious history. It set out in quest of the historical Jesus, believing that when it had found Him it could bring Him straight into our time as a Teacher and Saviour. It loosed the bands by which He had been riveted for centuries to the stony rock of ecclesiastical doctrine, and rejoiced to see life and movement coming into the figure once more, and the historical Jesus advancing, as it seemed, to meet it. But He does not stay; He passes by our time and returns to His own. What surprised and dismayed the theology of the last forty years was that, despite all forced and arbitrary interpretations, it could not keep Him in our time, but had to let Him go. He returned to His own time, not owing to the application of any historical ingenuity, but by the same inevitable necessity by which the liberated pendulum returns to its original position." (Q. 397.)

3. The Recorded Life of Jesus covers only a few months

"The 'Life of Jesus' is limited to the last months of his existence on earth. At the season of the summer seed-sowing he began his ministry and ended it upon the cross at Easter of the following year.

"His public ministry may be counted in weeks. The first period extends from seed time to harvest; the second comprises the days of his appearance in Jerusalem. Autumn and winter he spent in heathen territory alone with his Disciples." (M. 253.)

Again he says,

"Jesus spoke at the season of the seed-sowing and expected the Kingdom at the time of the harvest. Nature was God's clock. With the last seed-sowing he had set it for the last time." (M. 256.)

13

And once more,

"A very little consideration suffices to show that there is something quite incomprehensible in the public ministry of Jesus taken as a whole. According to Mark it lasted less than a year, for since he speaks of only one Passover-journey we may conclude that no other Passover fell within the period of Jesus' activity as a teacher. If it is proposed to assume that He allowed a Passover to go by without going up to Jerusalem, His adversaries, who took Him to task about hand-washings and about rubbing the ears of corn on the Sabbath, would certainly have made a most serious matter of this, and we should have to suppose that the Evangelist for some reason or other thought fit to suppress the fact. That is to say, the burden of proof lies upon those who assert a longer duration for the ministry of Jesus." (Q. 350.)

And he adds,

"This work of preaching the Kingdom was continued until the sending forth of the Twelve; that is to say, at the most for a few weeks. Perhaps in the saying 'the harvest is great but the labourers are few,' with which Jesus closes His work prior to sending forth the disciples, there lies an allusion to the actual state of the natural fields." (Q. 350.)

4. The Words of Jesus should much more often be taken literally than has been the custom in mediæval and conventional theology.

It has been too commonly taught that our Lord's words were used by him in a non-natural sense and that they carry

14

secret meanings highly charged with interpretations agreeable to the theology of the Fathers and of mediæval Saints. Against this Schweitzer asserts boldly that the words of Jesus usually carry their natural meaning and indicate just what he had in mind, and that this is especially true in His eschatological passages, for His whole mind was deeply embedded in Jewish eschatology as shewn forth in the later prophets, in the book of Daniel and in the book of Enoch, and the like.

"No more successful has been the attempt to evade the problem by *sublimating* the eschatology, as though Jesus had translated the realistic conceptions of his time into spiritual terms by using them in a figurative sense. The work of Eric Haupt (*Die eschatologischen Aussagen Jesu in den synoptischen Evangelien*, 1895) is based upon this thought. But there is nothing to justify us in assuming that Jesus attached to his words a non-natural sense, whereas his hearers, in accordance with the prevailing view, must have understood them realistically. Not only are we at a loss for a rational explanation of such a method on Jesus' part, but he himself gives not the slightest hint of it." (м. 85.)

After these brief remarks regarding Albert Schweitzer's general stand-point we will turn in detail to his exposition of the life and thought and teaching of Jesus.

5. At the Baptism of Jesus the secret of His Life was revealed to him.

"About Jesus' earlier development we know nothing. All lies in the dark. Only this is sure: at his baptism the secret of His existence was disclosed to Him—namely, that he was the one whom God had destined to be the Messiah." (M. 254.)

> 6. *Jesus as a learned Jew was deeply versed in Jewish Eschatology and Apocalyptic and on this His own religious thought was evidently based.*

We may recall the story in St. Luke's Gospel of the encounter between the boy Jesus and the Doctors in the Temple.

"The original and profound moral nature of Jesus took possession of the late-Jewish Eschatology and so gave expression, in the thought material of the age, to the hope and the will which are intent upon the ethical consummation of the world. All attempts to avert one's vision from this *Weltanschauung* as a whole and to make Jesus' significance for us to consist in His revelation of the 'fatherhood of God,' the 'brotherhood of man,' and so forth, must therefore of necessity lead to a narrow and peculiarly insipid conception of His religion. In reality He is an authority for us, not in the sphere of knowledge, but only in the matter of the will." (M. 49–50.)

In His preaching of the Kingdom of God Jesus felt certain of the closely approaching metamorphosis of the transcendental New Age. Here repentance was central: in this He was in line with the Baptist.

"The New Morality as Repentance. If the thought of the eschatological realisation of the Kingdom is the fundamental factor in Jesus' preaching, his whole theory of ethics must come under the conception of *repentance* as a preparation for the coming of the Kingdom." (M. 94.)

The Old Testament conception of Repentance and a new moral life and that set forth by Jesus in the Synoptic Gospels are alike.

"Both have a forward vision, both are dominated by the thought of a condition of perfection which God will bring to pass through the Judgment. This, in the Prophetic view, is the Day of the Lord; in the Synoptic it is the dawn of the Kingdom." (M. 95.)

"Jesus' ethics is closely connected with that of the Old Testament prophets, inasmuch as both are alike conditioned by the expectation of a state of perfection which God is to bring about. But also the secret of the Kingdom of God, according to which the moral renewal hastens the supernatural coming of the Kingdom, corresponds with the fundamental thought of the Prophets." (M. 112–3.)

"Jesus no longer conceives of it (the final event) as an intervention of God in the history of the Nations, as did the Prophets; but rather as a final cosmical catastrophe. His eschatology is the apocalyptic of the book of Daniel, since the Kingdom is to be brought about by the Son of Man when he appears upon the clouds of heaven (Mark viii. 38, ix. 1).

"The secret of the Kingdom of God is therefore the synthesis effected by a sovereign spirit between the early prophetic ethics and the apocalyptic of the book of Daniel. Hence it is that Jesus' eschatology was rooted in His age and yet stands so high above it." (M. 114–5.)

"A further point to be noticed is that the eschatology of

the time of Jesus shows the influence of the eschatology of the ancient prophets in a way which is not paralleled either before or after." (Q. 367.)

"But even in individual conceptions the apocalyptic of the Baptist, and of the period which he introduces, reaches back to the eschatology of the prophetic writings. The pouring forth of the spirit, and the figure of Elias, who comes again to earth, play a great role in it. The difficulty is, indeed, consciously felt of combining the two eschatologies, and bringing the prophetic within the Danielic." (Q. 367.)

Albert Schweitzer illuminates for us the situation in Jewish thought at the time, thus:

"What is really remarkable about this wave of apocalyptic enthusiasm is the fact that it was called forth not by external events, but solely by the appearance of two great personalities, and subsides with their disappearance, without leaving among the people generally any trace, except a feeling of hatred towards the new sect." (Q. 368.)

In one of the greatest passages in world literature Schweitzer thus portrays Jesus:

"There is silence all around. The Baptist appears, and cries: 'Repent, for the Kingdom of Heaven is at hand.' Soon after that comes Jesus, and in the knowledge that He is the coming Son of Man lays hold of the wheel of the world to set it moving on that last revolution, which is to bring all ordinary history to a close. It refuses to turn, and He throws Himself upon it. Then it does turn; and crushes Him. Instead of bringing in the eschatological conditions, He has destroyed them. The wheel rolls onward, and the mangled body of the one immeasurably great Man, who was strong

18

enough to think of Himself as the spiritual ruler of mankind and to bend history to His purpose, is hanging upon it still. That is His victory and His reign." (Q. 368-9.)

7. *Jesus as a Teacher. Why He spoke in Parables.*

Schweitzer maintains that, except in respect of *Inter-ims-ethik* (see below, section 18) Jesus had mainly in mind teaching concerning the closely impending Kingdom of God, the unimagineable change which He was certain was about to come upon the world, as foretold by Jewish apocalyptic.

"His life at this period was dominated by a 'dogmatic idea' which rendered Him indifferent to all else . . . . . even to the happy and successful work as a teacher which was opening before Him." (Q. 351.)

"His action suggests a doubt whether He really felt Himself to be a "teacher." If all the controversial discourses and sayings and answers to questions, which were so to speak wrung from Him, were subtracted from the sum of His utterances, how much of the didactic preaching of Jesus would be left over?" (Q. 351.)

"But even the supposed didactic preaching is not really that of a 'teacher,' since the purpose of His parables was, according to Mark iv. 10-12, not to reveal, but to conceal, and of the Kingdom of God He spoke only in parables (Mark iv. 34)." (Q. 351.)

And further:

"In the Synoptical accounts where is there even the slightest hint that Jesus wished to educate the Disciples and the people up to a knowledge of his messiahship?" (M. 4.)

What Jesus was chiefly concerned in is thus expressed by Schweitzer in relation to the parables about seed and leaven:—

"These parables are not at all devised to be interpreted and understood; rather they are calculated to make the hearers observant of the fact that in the affairs of the Kingdom of God a secret is preparing like that which they experience in nature. They are *signals*. As the harvest follows upon the seed-sowing, without it being possible for any one to say how it comes about; so, as the sequel to Jesus' preaching, will the Kingdom of God come with power." (M. 109.)

"They (His disciples) ought to have the presentiment that the moral renewal in consequence of his preaching stands in a necessary but inexplicable connection with the dawning of the Kingdom of God. The same God who through his mysterious power in nature brings the harvest to pass will also bring to pass the Kingdom of God.

"Therefore, when it was the season of the harvest, he sent His Disciples forth to proclaim: The Kingdom of God is at hand." (M. 110.)

And thus does Schweitzer throw light on a dark saying:—

"It should be observed that Jesus in these parables, as well as in the related saying at the sending forth of the Twelve, uses the formula, 'He that hath ears to hear, let him hear' (Mark iv. 23, and Matthew xi. 15), thereby signifying that in this utterance there lies concealed a supernatural knowledge concerning the plans of God, which only those who have ears to hear—that is, the fore-ordained—can detect. For others these sayings are unintelligible." (Q. 356.)

8. *The Predestinarianism of Jesus.*

And here it becomes necessary to set forth an aspect of our Lord of a kind less easily acceptable to His followers to-day. When the writer was a young school-boy he too was disturbed by St. Mark iv. 11–12. Not until he read Schweitzer was he given the explanation.

"Accordingly the fact of His always speaking in parables and of His taking this inexplicable resolution both point back to a mysterious pre-supposition which greatly reduces the importance of Jesus' work as a teacher.

"One reason for this limitation is distinctly stated in Mark iv. 10–12, *viz.* predestination! Jesus knows that the truth which He offers is exclusively for those who have been definitely chosen, that the general and public announcement of His message could only thwart the plans of God, since the chosen are already winning their salvation from God. Only the phrase, 'Repent for the Kingdom of God is at hand' and its variants belong to the public preaching. And this, therefore, is the only message which He commits to His disciples when sending them forth. What this repentance, supplementary to the law, the special ethic of the interval before the coming of the Kingdom (*Interims-ethik*) is, in its positive acceptation, He explains in the Sermon on the Mount. But all that goes beyond that simple phrase must be publicly presented only in parables, in order that those only, who are shown to possess predestination by having the initial knowledge which enables them to understand the parables, may receive a more advanced knowledge, which is imparted to them in a measure corresponding to their original degree of knowledge: 'Unto him that hath shall be given, and from him that hath not shall be taken away even that which he hath" (Mark iv. 24–25). (Q. 352.)

The following, however, must never be forgotten:—

"But the ethical idea of salvation and the predestinarian limitation of acceptance to the elect are constantly in conflict in the mind of Jesus." (Q. 353.)

Continuing:—

"Predestinarianism, in fact, dominated the thoughts of Jesus. The Lord is conscious that He dies only for the elect. For others His death can avail nothing, nor even their own repentance. Moreover, He does not die in order that this one or that one may come into the Kingdom of God: He provides the atonement in order that the Kingdom itself may come. Until the Kingdom comes even the elect cannot possess it." (Q. 388.)

St. Paul's thought, too, is dominated by the idea of predestination. Not man as such but only the man who is elected can enter into relation with God.

"The man in the parable of the Royal Marriage who sits down among the guests but has no wedding-garment is one who has followed the call, without being predestined." (MP. 102.)

"To belong to the community of those who are called to the fellowship of the Son of Man annuls all other relationships. To those who tell Him that His mother and brethren are asking for Him, Jesus declares, with a glance at the believers who surround Him, that these are His mother and His brethren, because they are resolved to do the will of God (Mark iii. 31–35). In the discourse at the sending out of the disciples He declares uncompromisingly that love of father, mother, brothers, and sisters must take second place to love

of Himself (Matthew x. 37), the thought being that by love
to Him a man enters the fellowship of the Son of Man and
His followers." (MP. 108.)

And again as between Jews and Gentiles:

"The privilege of entering upon the rights of the Elect by
a free choice is reserved to the Children of Israel. This explains how it is that Jesus is universalistic in His thinking and
Jewish-particularistic in His action." (MP. 180.)

With reference to St. John's Gospel:

"It is worthy of note that the Gospel of John regards the
Jewish people as such, with the exception of a few individuals, as hostile to the Logos." (MP. 351.)

Regarding the Beatitudes, Schweitzer writes:

"It may seem to us inconceivable, but they are really predestinarian in form. Blessed are the poor in spirit! Blessed
are the meek! Blessed are the peacemakers!—that does not
mean that by virtue of their being poor in spirit, meek,
peace-loving, they deserve the Kingdom. Jesus does not in-
tend the saying as an injunction or exhortation, but as a
simple statement of fact: in their being poor in spirit, in their
meekness, in their love of peace, it is made manifest that they
are predestined to the Kingdom. By the possession of those
qualities they are marked as belonging to it. In the case of
others (Matthew v. 10–12) the predestination to the Kingdom is made manifest by the persecutions which befall them
in this world. These are the light of the world, which already
shines among men for the glory of God (Matthew v. 14–15).

"The kingdom cannot be 'earned'; what happens is that
men are called to it, and show themselves to be called to
it." (Q. 353.)

9. His "Galilean Springtime" and its Aftermath.

Schweitzer maintains that the period of our Lord's life and teaching, which has been thus happily termed, was in fact a period not of success but of humiliation and ill-success. He believes that Jesus expected the coming of the Kingdom by the next harvest time. He was astonished that in His native town there were so few believers, *i.e.* elect, since He expected the Kingdom of God any moment. His departure to the Capital became inevitable. Notwithstanding the "Galilean springtime" matters had not gone well:

"Already in Mark iii. 6 it has come to the point of a murderous attack. Jesus has to renounce his family because they wish to fetch him home by force as one who is mentally incompetent (Mark iii. 20–22, 31–35). At Nazareth he is rejected (Mark vi. 1–6)." (M. 64.)

And there must have been further reasons,

"The hints also which he drops at that time in the presence of the people point to bitter catastrophes. What must have occurred in Chorazin, in Capernaum, and in Bethsaida that he calls down upon them the wrath of the Day of Judgment, in which it shall be more tolerable for Tyre and Sidon than for them (Matthew xi. 20–24)!" (M. 65–6.)

But after the return of the apostles there was neither growing opposition nor widespread defection.

"By means of their preaching and their signs the reputation of his mighty personality spread far and wide. Now begins the time of success!" (M. 260.)

"It will now be perfectly clear how unhistoric is the view that Jesus left Galilee in consequence of growing opposition and spreading defection. On the contrary, this is the period

24

of his highest triumph. A multitude of people with faith in the Kingdom thronged him and pursued him everywhere. Hardly had he landed upon the west coast but they are already there. Their number has grown still greater and increases more and more (Mark vi. 53, 56). That they deserted him, that they even showed the least motion of doubt or defection, the texts give no intimation. *It was not the people that deserted Jesus but Jesus that deserted the people.*

"This he did, not out of any fear of the emissaries from Jerusalem, but only as carrying out what he already had in mind since the return of the Disciples. He wishes to be alone." (M. 178–9.)

10. His Concealment of His Messiahship.

Dr. Schweitzer begins in *The Mystery of the Kingdom of God* with these questions:

"If Jesus really regarded himself as Messiah, how comes it that he acted as if he were not Messiah?"

"In the Synoptical accounts where is there even the slightest hint that Jesus wished to educate the Disciples and the people up to a knowledge of his Messiahship?"

"Why did Jesus never try through instruction to raise the people up to the new ethical conception of messiahship? The attempt would not have been so hopeless as one commonly assumes, for at that time there was a deep spiritual movement going on in Israel. Why did Jesus maintain persistent silence about his conception of Messiahship?" (M. 4–5.)

This at least Schweitzer is sure of:

"Up to the time of the mission of the Twelve no one had the faintest idea of recognising in him the Messiah. At Cæsarea Philippi the Disciples could only reply that the people took him for a prophet or for Elijah the Forerunner, and they themselves knew no better, for Peter, as Jesus himself said, did not derive his knowledge from the Master's ministry in work and word, but owed it to a supernatural revelation." (M. 127–8.)

But we learn that some suspected his Messiahship, because "Messiah" and "Son of God" have the same meaning, and would recall to everyone the book of Daniel (Daniel vii. 13).

"Matthew xii. 23: After a miraculous healing the people whisper to themselves whether this is not the Son of David.

"Matthew xiv. 33: After their experience at sea in the boat the Disciples fall down before him, saying, 'Truly thou art the Son of God.'

"Matthew xv. 22: The Canaanitish woman addressed him as the Son of David,—whereas according to Mark she simply falls at his feet and cries for help."

And similarly the demoniacs:

"According to Mark iii. 11 the unclean spirits, as often as they saw him, threw themselves at his feet and addressed him as the Son of God (cf. also Mark i. 24). It is true, he rebuked this cry and commanded silence. But if we did not have the incontestably sure information that during the whole of his Galilean ministry the people knew no more than that he was a prophet or Elijah, we should be forced to assume that these cries of the demoniacs made the people somehow aware of his true character. As it is, however, we may discern with precision, from the fact that the demon-

26

cries were ignored, how very far men were from suspecting him to be the Messiah." (M. 128–9.)

When was it first that Jesus alluded to himself before His disciples as "Son of Man?" We cannot be sure. But in His last days in Jerusalem neither the scribes nor the people thought of Him as a Messianic personality but merely a great prophet. But somehow (we shall see how later) the High Priest got to know what His claim was before His trial, for he asked the vital question outright. But on His entry into Jerusalem did the people give Him a Messianic ovation? Again, we cannot be sure. But on the mount of Transfiguration it was in a state of ecstacy that the three chosen disciples learnt in their talk His great secret and it was at Cæsarea Philippi that the confession of Peter told the stupendous announcement to all the other apostles, including Judas.

In fact Jesus used the title "Son of Man" commonly in the third person and with a futuristic sense. No one regarded Him as a Messiah—only with regard to the Entry into Jerusalem does some doubt still remain. Yet the 4th Gospel speaks of him as if he had come upon earth as the Messiah.

Finally and to sum up:

"We have therefore three revelations of the secret of Messiahship, which so hang together that each subsequent one implies the foregoing. On the mountain near Bethsaida was revealed to the Three the secret which was disclosed to Jesus at his baptism. That was after the harvest.[1] A few weeks later it was known to the Twelve, by the fact that Peter at Cæsarea Philippi answered Jesus' question out of the knowledge which he had attained upon the mountain.

[1] Dr. Schweitzer's argument against the Synoptics who place Caesarea Philippi *before* the Transfiguration is given on p. 36.

One of the Twelve betrayed the secret to the High Priest. This last revelation of the secret was fatal, for it brought about the death of Jesus. *He was condemned as Messiah although He had never appeared in that role.*" (M. 217–8.).

11. *The Mission of the Twelve. Matthew X. 23.*

This Dr. Schweitzer calls a decisive text. It is clearly central to his whole position and is supported by many texts of the same kind. Mainly upon this text he tells what he believes was the great expectation of Jesus, an expectation which however was never fulfilled. I will quote at full length from *The Mystery of the Kingdom of God.*

" 'The Kingdom of God is at hand' (Matthew x. 7)—this word which Jesus commissions his Disciples to proclaim is a summary expression of all his previous preaching. They are to carry it now throughout the cities of Israel. The charge of Jesus to the Twelve furnishes no means of determining in what sense this proclamation is meant.

"If the common conception is right about the significance of this mission of the Twelve, the words with which he dismisses them present an extraordinary riddle. Full of hope and with the joy of productive effort he goes about to extend the scope of his activity for the founding of the Kingdom of God. The commission of the Twelve ought therefore to contain instruction about the missionary propaganda they were to carry out in this sense. One must hence expect that he would direct them how they should preach about

28

the new relation to God and the new morality of the King-dom.

"The commission, however, is anything but a summary of the 'teaching of Jesus.' It does not in the least contemplate instruction of a thoroughgoing kind, rather what is in question is a flying proclamation throughout Israel. The one errand of the Apostles as teachers is to cry out everywhere the warning of the nearness of the Kingdom of God—to the intent that all may be warned and given opportunity to repent. In this, however, no time is to be lost; therefore they are not to linger in a town where men are unsusceptible to their message, but to hasten on in order that they may pass through all the cities of Israel before the appearing of the Son of Man takes place. But 'the coming of the Son of Man' signifies—*the dawning of the Kingdom of God with power.*

"When they persecute you in this city flee unto another, for verily I say unto you, Ye shall not have gone through the cities of Israel till the Son of Man be come (Matthew x. 23). If one so understands the commission of the Twelve as to suppose that Jesus would say through his Disciples that the time is now come for the realisation of the Kingdom by a new moral behaviour, that eschatological saying lies like an erratic boulder in the midst of a flowery meadow. If, however, one conceives of the embassage eschatologically, the saying acquires a great context: it is a rock in the midst of a wild mountain landscape. One cannot affirm of this saying that it has been interpolated here by a later age; rather with compelling force it fixes the presence of eschatological conceptions in the days of the mission of the Twelve." (M. 87–89.)

Jesus goes on to warn His messengers of the sufferings which lie ahead of them.

"The secular authority will bring upon them severe persecution (Matthew x. 17, 31). Men will call them to account and subject them to torture in order to move them to denial of their cause. Brother shall deliver up brother to death, and the father his child; and children shall rise up against parents and cause them to be put to death. Only he who remains steadfast in the midst of this general tumult, and confesses Jesus before men, shall be saved in the Day of Judgment, when he intervenes with God in their behalf (Matthew x. 32, 33)." (M. 91.)

Moreover, Jesus has in mind only salvation for the Jews,

"Go not into any way of the Gentiles, and enter not into any city of the Samaritans: but go rather to the lost sheep of the house of Israel." (M. 117.)

But Schweitzer adds,

"The preaching of the Kingdom of God is therefore particularistic; the Kingdom itself, however, is universalistic, 'for they shall come from the east and from the west, from the north and from the south.'"

What was the actual outcome and how did Jesus meet it?

"Hitherto he had spoken only in general terms of the final Affliction as an event of the last times. Now, however, it has been fulfilled upon the Baptist as an *historical event*. That is a sign, which indicates how it will be fulfilled upon himself.

"This indication came precisely at the time when he was compelled by the course of events to reflect upon the final Affliction. After the return of the Twelve he had expected it as an impending event. But it failed to occur. What is more, the Kingdom failed therewith to appear! In sending out the

Twelve he had told them that they would be surprised by the overflowing woes ere they had gone through all the cities of Israel,—and they had returned without witnessing the beginning of the woes or the dawn of the Kingdom.

"The report with which they returned showed, however, that all was ready. Already the power of ungodliness was broken, for else the unclean spirits would not have been subject to them. The Kingdom was compellingly hastened by the repentance practised since the days of the Baptist. In this respect also the measure was full,—that was proved by the multitudes which thronged about him in faithful expectation. So all was ready—and still the Kingdom did not come! The delay of the eschatological coming of the Kingdom,—that was the great fact which drove Jesus at that time once and again into solitude to seek light upon the mystery." (M. 233–4.)

And Schweitzer thus views the effect upon Gospel tradition consequent upon the failure of this vision:

"The Kingdom which Jesus expected so very soon failed to make its appearance. This first eschatological delay and postponement was momentous for the fate of the Gospel tradition, inasmuch as now all the events related to the mission of the Twelve became unintelligible, because all consciousness was lost of the fact that the most intense eschatological expectation then inspired Jesus and his following." (M. 264.)

And following upon the mission and consequent on its failure Jesus seeks solitude to understand that failure by pondering upon two Messianic facts. He seeks answers to these two questions and these are the answers He seems to obtain:

"Why is the Baptist executed by the secular authority before the Messianic time has dawned?

"Why does the Kingdom fail to appear notwithstanding that the tokens of its dawning are present?

"The secret is made known to him through the Scripture: God brings the Kingdom about *without the general Affliction.* He whom God has destined to reign in glory accomplishes it upon himself by being tried as a malefactor and condemned. Wherefore the others go free: he makes the atonement for them. What though they believe that God punishes him, though they become offended in him who preached unto them righteousness,—when after his Passion the glory dawns, then shall they see that he has suffered for them.

"Thus Jesus read in the Prophet Isaiah what God had determined for him, the Elect." (M. 264–5.)

For Schweitzer insists (*The Quest,* p. 357) that Jesus lived wholly for dogmatic history. And He is confronted with an expected event of supernatural history which has failed to come about.

"The whole history of 'Christianity' down to the present day, that is to say, the real inner history of it, is based on the delay of the Parousia, the non-occurrence of the Parousia, and abandonment of eschatology, the progress and completion of the 'de-eschatologising' of religion which has been connected therewith. It should be noted that the non-fulfilment of Matthew x. 23 is the first postponement of the Parousia. We have therefore here the first significant date in the 'history of Christianity'; it gives to the work of Jesus a new direction, otherwise inexplicable." (Q. 358.)

And further:

"Jesus' purpose is to set in motion the eschatological development of history, to let loose the final woes, the confusion and strife, from which shall issue the Parousia, and so to introduce the supra-mundane phrase of the eschatological drama. That is His task, for which He has authority here below. That is why He says in the same discourse, 'Think not that I am come to send peace on the earth; I am not come to send peace, but a sword.' (Matthew x. 34.)

"It was with a view to this initial movement that He chose His disciples. They are not His helpers in the work of teaching; we never see them in that capacity, and He did not prepare them to carry on that work after His death. The very fact that He chooses just twelve shows that it is a dogmatic idea which He has in mind. He chooses them as those who are destined to hurl the firebrand into the world, and are afterwards, as those who have been the comrades of the unrecognised Messiah, before He came to His Kingdom, to be His associates in ruling and judging it." (Q. 369.)

Schweitzer delineates with utmost care his conception of the expectation of Jesus when the Twelve are sent out (Matthew x.).

". . . . Jesus predicts to the disciples in the same discourse that to their own surprise a supernatural wisdom will suddenly speak from their lips, so that it will be not they but the Spirit of God who will answer the great ones of the earth. As the Spirit is for Jesus and early Christian theology something concrete which is to descend upon the elect among mankind only in consequence of a definite event— the outpouring of the Spirit which, according to the prophecy of Joel, should precede the day of judgment—Jesus must have anticipated that this would occur during the absence

33

of the disciples, in the midst of the time of strife and confusion.

"To put it differently; the whole of the discourse at the
sending forth of the Twelve, taken in the clear sense of the
words, is a prediction of the events of the 'time of the End,'
events which are immediately at hand, in which the supernatural eschatological course of history will break through
into the natural course. The expectation of sufferings is
therefore doctrinal and unhistorical, as is, precisely in the
same way, the expectation of the pouring forth of the Spirit
uttered at the same time. The Parousia of the Son of Man is
to be preceded according to the Messianic dogma by a time
of strife and confusion—as it were, the birth-throes of the
Messiah—and the outpouring of the Spirit. It should be
noticed that according to Joel ii and iii the outpouring of the
Spirit, along with the miraculous signs, forms the prelude to
the judgment; and also, that in the same context, Joel iii. 13,
the judgment is described as the harvest-day of God." (Q.
360-1.)

And from the Old Testament:

"A general pouring out of the Spirit and prophesying,
wonders in heaven and upon earth,—all that was to occur before the Day of God comes. So it was defined by the prophet
Joel (ii. 28 ff.). Peter in his sermon at Pentecost appealed to
this passage (Acts ii. 17-22). One ought to recognise from the
supernatural ecstatic 'tongues' that one is approaching the
end of the days. The crucified Jesus hath God raised up to
be the Messiah in the Resurrection, and the Kingdom will
soon dawn.

"This passage in Joel was therefore applied to the time immediately preceding the messianic age, the time of miracles,

34

in which according to the prophecy of Malachi the Forerunner should appear (Malachi iii. 4.). Moreover, the self-same refrain unites these two fundamental passages of pre-Messianic expectation: Malachi iv. 5 is the same as Joel ii. 31— 'Before the coming of the great and terrible Day of the Lord.' *The Forerunner without miracles in an unmiraculous age was therefore unthinkable.*" (M. 140–1.)

A conception clearly shared by St. Peter in Acts, and again in Daniel.

"Daniel xii. 1: 'And at that time shall Michael arise, a great Prince which standeth for the children of thy people, and there shall be a time of trouble such as never was since there was a nation even to that time, but at that time thy people shall be delivered, every one that shall be found written in the book.'

"The idea that the saints who are destined to the Kingdom are all inscribed in the Book of Life appears thenceforward again and again in eschatology (Psalm lxix. 29; Daniel xii. 1; Enoch ciii. 2, civ. 1, cviii. 3). According to the Psalms of Solomon they bear God's mark upon them, which safeguards them when the wrath of God goes forth to destroy the ungodly (Ps. Sol. xv. 4–6)." (MP. 102).

12. *The Transfiguration.*

"Coming *after* Cæsarea Philippi the Transfiguration is an obscure episode devoid of historical significance. The Three learn no more about Jesus than Peter had already confessed in the presence of the Twelve and Jesus himself had confirmed. Thus the whole section is plainly an intrusion: the

apotheosis and obscure dialogue have no historical significance."

Dr. Schweitzer holds that the Synoptics are wrong in placing Cæsarea Philippi *before* the Transfiguration. He
writes:—

"If, however, as has been proved by literary evidence, this
scene was enacted some weeks *after* the mission of the
Twelve and *before* Cæsarea Philippi—not upon the mountain of the legend, but on the mountain in the lonely region
by the seashore near Bethsaida,—then we behold an idle ad-
dendum transformed at one stroke into a Galilean occurrence of far reaching historical importance, which explains
the scene at Cæsarea Philippi, and not *vice versa*. What we
call the Transfiguration is in reality nothing else but the
revelation of the secret of messiahship to the Three. A few
weeks later comes then its disclosure to the Twelve." (M.
180–1.)

"Peter knew that Jesus is the 'Son of God' through the
revelation which he in common with the two other Disciples
received on the mountain near Bethsaida. For this reason he
answered the question with such confidence (Mark viii. 29)."
(M. 183.)

It was perhaps in a state of ecstasy, similar, Dr. Schweitzer
suggests, to the conditions at our Lord's Baptism, and to St.
Paul's at Damascus Gate, that He saw and heard the appear-
ances of Moses and Elias and the voices in the clouds. It was
there that Three of His Disciples first knew the secret of His
Messiahship.

"There is in fact an inward connection between the Baptism and the Transfiguration. In both cases a condition of
ecstacy accompanies the revelation of the secret of Jesus'

person. The first time the revelation was for him alone; here the Disciples also share it. It is not clear to what extent they themselves were transported by the experience. So much is sure, that in a dazed condition, out of which they awake only at the end of the scene (Mark ix. 8), the figure of Jesus appears to them illuminated by a supernatural light and glory, and a voice intimates that he is the Son of God. The occurrence can be explained only as the outcome of great eschatological excitement." (M. 181–2.)

13. *The Confession of Peter at Caesarea Philippi.*

"Blessed art thou, Simon Bar-Jonah: for flesh and blood hath not revealed it unto thee, but my Father which is in heaven" (Matthew xvi. 17).

These are the ever-famous words with which St. Peter here is addressed by our Lord. Dr. Schweitzer continues:

"The scene which follows upon Peter's answer clearly has to do with a secret common to him and to Jesus. When Jesus disclosed that he must die in Jerusalem Peter turns upon him impetuously, takes him apart, and speaks to him in excited tones. As Jesus sees that the other Disciples are attentive he abruptly turns away from Peter with a sharp word, calling him the Tempter, who minds not the things of God but the things of men (Mark viii. 32, 33)." (M. 183.)

"Only from the point of view of the eschatological doctrine of redemption does it become intelligible why Jesus, when Peter seeks to dissuade Him from His purpose of dying, hears in his voice the voice of Satan. For Satan has an interest in His giving up that purpose. If Jesus does not die the dominion of the Evil One will continue." (MP. 61.)

"Why this agitation of Peter over Jesus' disclosure about the fatal journey to Jerusalem? Because it comes as a new factor, above and beyond what was disclosed on the mountain near Bethsaida. About that experience he dare not speak in the presence of the other Disciples, because Jesus had forbidden it. For this reason he takes Jesus apart. Jesus, however, seeing that the other Disciples are listening, cannot explain matters to him, and so with passionate abruptness enjoins silence." (M. 183–4.)

"Taken by itself the whole scene at Cæsarea Philippi is an enigma. If, however, we assume that the Transfiguration preceded it, the enigma is solved and the scene is illuminated down to the smallest details. The revelation to the Twelve was preceded by the disclosure to the Three of the secret of Jesus' Messiahship." (M. 184–5.)

"At Cæsarea Philippi it is not He, but Peter, who reveals His Messiahship. We may say, therefore, that Jesus did not voluntarily give up His Messianic secret; it was wrung from Him by the pressure of events." (Q. 384.)

And Schweitzer speaks thus of our Lord's foretellings at Cæsarea Philippi of his coming sufferings:

"In order to understand Jesus' resolve to suffer, we must first recognize that the mystery of this suffering is involved in the mystery of the Kingdom of God, since the Kingdom cannot come until the πειϱαμιος has taken place. This certainty of suffering is quite independent of the historic circumstances, as the beatitude on the persecuted in the sermon on the mount, and the predictions in the discourse at the sending forth of the Twelve, clearly show. Jesus' predic-

38

tion of His own sufferings at Cæsarea Philippi is precisely as unintelligible, precisely as dogmatic, and therefore precisely as historical as the prediction to the disciples at the time of their mission. The 'must be' of the sufferings is the same—the coming of the Kingdom, and of the Parousia, which are dependent upon the πειραμος having first taken place." (Q. 385.)

"What is certain is that, for Him, suffering was always associated with the Messianic secret, since He places His Parousia at the end of the pre-Messianic tribulations in which He was to have His part." (Q. 386.)

And finally:

"In the secret of His passion which Jesus reveals to the disciples at Cæsarea Philippi, the pre-Messianic tribulation is for others set aside, abolished, concentrated upon Himself alone, and that in the form that they are fulfilled in His own passion and death at Jerusalem. That was the new conviction that had dawned upon Him. He must suffer for others that the Kingdom might come." (Q. 386-7.)

14. The questions put by the Baptist and the beginning of the Pre-Messianic period.

"Jesus was alone. The Disciples carried the news of the nearness of the Kingdom throughout the cities of Israel." (M. 110.)

"He had just sent out His Disciples and given them to expect that the appearing of the Son of Man might surprise them on their way through the cities of Israel. The hour is already far more advanced—that is what Jesus would give the people to understand in his 'eulogy over the Baptist,' if they can receive it.

"John reached this surmise about Jesus in the same way as did the people. That is to say, as he heard *of the signs and deeds of Jesus* (Matthew xi. 2), there occurred to him the thought that this might be something more than a prophet with a call to repentance. So he sends messengers to him in order to have assurance upon this point." (M. 150–1.)

"While the people thronged him there came the emissaries of the Baptist with their question." (Matthew xi. 2–6.)

"Now when John had heard in the prison the words of Christ, he sent two of his disciples,

"And said unto him, Art thou he that should come, or do we look for another?

"Jesus answered and said unto them, Go and show John again those things which ye do hear and see:

"The blind receive their sight, and the lame walk, the lepers are cleansed, and the deaf hear, the dead are raised up, and the poor have the gospel preached to them.

"And blessed is he, whosoever shall not be offended in me."

"He dismissed them with the answer: the Kingdom stands before the door, one needs only the language of the signs and wonders in order to understand. Turning to the people he speaks of the significance of the Baptist and of his office. With this he lets drop a hint of mystery (Matthew xi. 14, 'If you are able to conceive it,' Matthew xi. 15, 'he that hath ears to hear, let him hear'). John is Elijah, *i.e.* the personality whose advent marks the immediate dawning of the Kingdom." (Malachi iv. 5.)

Matthew xi. 13, 14, 15 are key words in the eschatology of Jesus. The verses in Malachi iii. 1 and iv. 5 are ever in his mind.

"How much he was pre-occupied with the thought of the Baptist's death is shown by the conversation which followed the revelation to the Three on the mountain. It was ordained in the Scripture that Elijah must meet such a fate at the hands of men. So also it is written of the Son of Man that He must suffer many things and be set at naught (Mark ix. 12, 13)." (M. 233.)

Further Schweitzer points out to us in a footnote in *The Quest* that we can here see how short a time before the death of the Baptist the ministry of Jesus had begun.

"He only became known, as the Baptist's question shows, at the time of the mission of the disciples; Herod first heard of Him after the death of the Baptist. Had he known anything of Jesus beforehand, it would have been impossible for him suddenly to identify Him with the Baptist risen from the dead. This elementary calculation has been overlooked in all calculations of the length of the public ministry of Jesus." (Q. 371.)

"Jesus cannot tell him (John) who he is. 'The time is far advanced'—that is the gist of his reply. After the departure of the messengers Jesus turned to the people and signified in mysterious terms that the time is indeed much further advanced than the Baptist dreamed in asking such a question. The era of the Forerunner had already begun with the appearance of the Baptist himself. From that time on the Kingdom of God is with violence compelled to draw near. He himself who asks the question is Elijah—if they could

41

comprehend it. Men were not able to perceive that the man in prison was Elijah." (м. 260–1.)

"The fact was, the Baptist had put Him in an extremely difficult position. He could not answer that He was Elias if He held Himself to be the Messiah; on the other hand He could not, and would not, disclose to him, and still less to the messengers and the listening multitude, the secret of His Messiahship. Therefore He sends this obscure message, which only contains a confirmation of the facts which John had already heard and closes with a warning, come what may, not to be offended in Him. Of this the Baptist was to make what he could.

"It mattered, in fact, little how John understood the message. The time was much more advanced than he supposed; the hammer of the world's clock had risen to strike the last hour. All that he needed to know was that he had no cause to doubt.

"In revealing to the people the true office of the Baptist, Jesus unveiled to them almost the whole mystery of the Kingdom of God, and nearly disclosed the secret of His Messiahship. For if Elias was already present, was not the coming of the Kingdom close at hand? And if John was Elias, who was Jesus? . . . . There could only be one answer: the Messiah. But this seemed impossible, because Messiah was expected as a supernatural personality. The eulogy on the Baptist is, historically regarded, identical in content with the prediction of the Parousia in the discourse at the sending forth of the disciples. For after the coming of Elias there must follow immediately the judgment and the other events belonging to the last time. Now we can understand why in the enumeration of the events of the last time in the dis-

course to the Twelve the coming of Elias is not mentioned."
(Q. 373.)

Dr. Schweitzer continues:

"We see here, in the first place, the importance of the revelation which Jesus had made to the people in declaring to them the secret that the Baptist is Elias. From the standpoint of the eschatological expectation no one could recognise Elias in the Baptist, unless he knew of the Messiahship of Jesus. And no one could believe in the Messiahship and 'resurrection' of Jesus, that is, in His Parousia, without presupposing that Elias had in some way or other already come. This was therefore the primary difficulty of the disciples, the stumbling-block which Jesus must remove for them by making the same revelation concerning the Baptist to them as to the people. It is also once more abundantly clear that expectation was directed at that time primarily to the coming of Elias. It is to be noted that the cry of Jesus from the cross, 'Eli, Eli,' was immediately interpreted by the bystanders as referring to Elias." (Q. 381.)

From the days of the Baptist we stand immediately within the Messianic period.

15. Jesus warns His followers that the Last Times are at hand.

The time is far advanced.

"Disparagement of the earthly form of existence goes to the length of sacrificing altogether the earthly life for the sake of full assurance of life in the coming age. Hence, with the exhortation to follow him in suffering and reproach, Jesus declares that 'whosoever would save his life shall lose it.' That is to say, whosoever, through anxiety about his earthly existence, makes himself unworthy that the Son of Man intervene for him before God, forfeits thereby the Messianic life which commences with the Resurrection (Mark viii. 35)." (M. 207.)

Schweitzer further says:

"If we look into the thought more closely we see that the coming of the Kingdom of God is not only symbolically or analogically, but also really and temporarily connected with the harvest. The harvest ripening upon earth is the last! With it comes also the Kingdom of God which brings in the new age. When the reapers are sent into the fields, the Lord in Heaven will cause his harvest to be reaped by the holy angels.

"If the three parables of Mark iv. contain the mystery of the Kingdom of God, and are therefore capable of being summed up in a single formula, this can be nothing else than the joyful exhortation: 'Ye who have eyes to see, read in the harvest which is ripening upon earth, what is being prepared in heaven!' The eager eschatological hope was to regard the natural process as the last of its kind, and to see in it a special significance in view of the event of which it was to give the signal.

"The analogical and temporal parallelism becomes complete if we assume that the movement initiated by the Baptist began in the spring, and notice that Jesus, according to Matthew ix. 37 and 38, before sending out the disciples to make a speedy proclamation of the nearness of the Kingdom of God, uttered the remarkable saying about the rich har-

44

vest. It seems like a final expression of the thought contained in the parables about the seed and its promise, and finds its most natural explanation in the supposition that the harvest was actually at hand.

"Whatever may be thought of this attempt to divine historically the secret of the Kingdom of God, there is one thing that cannot be got away from, *viz.* that the initial fact to which Jesus points, under the figure of the sowing, is somehow or other connected with the eschatological preaching of repentance, which had been begun by the Baptist." (Q. 355.)

In footnotes in *The Quest* Schweitzer quotes from the Old Testament and from Apocalyptic writings:

"Joel iii. 13, 'Put in the sickle for the harvest is ripe!' In the Apocalypse of John, too, the Last Judgment is described as the heavenly harvest: 'Thrust in thy sickle and reap; for the time is come for thee to reap; for the harvest of the earth is ripe. And he that sat on the cloud thrust in his sickle on the earth; and the earth was reaped' (Revelation xiv. 15 and 16).

"The most remarkable parallel to the discourse at the sending forth of the disciples is offered by the Syrian Apocalypse of Baruch: 'Behold, the days come, when the time of the world shall be ripe, and the harvest of the sowing of the good and of the evil shall come, when the Almighty shall bring upon the earth and upon its inhabitants and upon their rulers confusion of spirit and terror that makes the heart stand still' . . . . .

"The connexion between the ideas of harvest and of judgment was therefore one of the stock features of the apocalyptic writings. And as the Apocalypse of Baruch dates from the period about A.D. 70, it may be assumed that this association of ideas was also current in the Jewish apocalyptic of the time of Jesus. Here is a basis for understanding the secret of the Kingdom of God in the parables of sowing and reaping historically and in accordance with the ideas of the time. What Jesus did was to make known to those who understood Him that the coming earthly harvest was the last, and was also the token of the coming heavenly harvest. The eschatological interpretation is immensely strengthened by these parallels." (q. 361.)

Parable after parable give the same warning, *e.g.* Matthew vii. 24–27, and also the parables of the treasure in the field, and of the pearl of great price.

16. *A state of eschatological expectation.*

"We must always make a fresh effort to realise to ourselves, that Jesus and His immediate followers were, at that time, in an enthusiastic state of intense eschatological expectation. We must picture them among the people, who were filled with penitence for their sins, and with faith in the Kingdom, hourly expecting the coming of the Kingdom, and the revelation of Jesus as the Son of Man, seeing in the eager multitude itself a sign that their reckoning of the time was correct; thus the psychological conditions were present for a common ecstatic experience such as is described in the account of the transfiguration." (q. 384.)

So too with the Sons of Zebedee on the last journey to Jerusalem. Dr. Schweitzer points out:

46

"On the way to Jerusalem the same scene was reenacted in closest conjunction with the third prediction of the Passion. (Mark x. 32–41.) The sons of Zebedee advance their claim to the seats upon the throne. This is not in the least a case of childish misunderstanding on the part of his followers, for Jesus in fact treats their suggestion with perfect seriousness. The eschatological expectation must accordingly have been thrown into such strong relief for the Disciples by Jesus' prediction of his Passion that they necessarily reasoned within themselves about the position they should occupy in the coming Kingdom." (M. 79.)

"For the loftier stations, however, it is necessary to have proved oneself in persecution and suffering. Accordingly, Jesus asks the sons of Zebedee whether, since they claim these thrones on His right hand and on His left, they feel themselves strong enough to drink of His cup and be baptized with His baptism (Mark x. 38.) To serve, to humble oneself, to incur persecution and death, belong to 'the ethic of the interim' just as much as does penitence. They are indeed only a higher form of penitence." (Q. 364.)

"From the saying in which He promises the Disciples that they shall sit upon twelve thrones, judging the twelve Tribes of Israel, we learn that the judgment of the Son of Man coincides with the 'Palingesia,' that is to say, the creation anew of the heaven and the earth (Matthew xix. 28)." (MP. 80.)

17. The Resurrection Foretellings.

"What is the significance of the resurrection-prophecies? It seems to us hard to admit that Jesus could have foretold

47

so precisely an event of that sort. It seems much more plausible to suppose that general utterances of his about a glory that awaited him were editorially transformed *ex eventu* into predictions of the Resurrection.

"Such criticism is in place so long as one holds the view that the prophecy of the Resurrection referred to an isolated event in the personal history of Jesus. So it appears, however, only to our modern consciousness, because we think uneschatologically even in the matter of the Resurrection. For Jesus and his Disciples, on the other hand, the Resurrection which he spoke about had an entirely different significance. It was a Messianic event which signified the dawn of the full glory that was to come. We must eliminate from the Resurrection predicted by Jesus all modern notions suggestive of an apotheosis. The contemporary consciousness understood this 'Restoration' (Acts iii. 21) as a revelation of Jesus' Messiahship at the dawn of the Kingdom. Therefore when Jesus spoke of his resurrection the Disciples thought of the great Messianic Resurrection in which he as the Messiah would be raised from the dead.

"The conversation during the descent from the mountain of Transfiguration is decisive on this point. Jesus spoke then for the first time to his most intimate disciples of 'the resurrection of the Son of Man' apart from the Messianic Resurrection. Their attention was entirely occupied with the Messianic event which Jesus' words suggested to them. They question therefore among themselves about the Resurrection of the dead. What should that mean (Mark ix. 10)? That is to say, the conditions thereof, so far as they can see, are not yet fulfilled. Elijah is not yet come (Mark ix. 11). Jesus puts their minds at rest with the hint that Elijah had already appeared though men did not recognise him. He means the Baptist (Mark ix. 12, 13)." (M. 201.)

And again:

"The 'Resurrection of the dead' was, in fine, only the mode in which the transformation of the whole form of existence was accomplished upon those who had already succumbed to death." (M. 205–6.)

In a later passage and footnote Dr. Schweitzer once more makes his point clear:

"A vivid eschatological expectation is therefore impossible to conceive apart from the idea of a metamorphosis. The resurrection is only a special case of this metamorphosis, the form in which the new condition of things is realised in the case of these who are already dead. The resurrection, the metamorphosis, and the Parousia of the Son of Man take place simultaneously, and are one and the same act." (Q. 304.)

And in a footnote:

"If, therefore, Jesus at a later point predicted to His disciples His resurrection, He means by that, not a single isolated act, but a complex occurrence consisting of His metamorphosis, translation to heaven, and Parousia as the Son of Man. And with this is associated the general eschatological resurrection of the dead. It is, therefore, one and the same thing whether He speaks of His resurrection or of His coming on the clouds of heaven." (Q. 364.)

Nor is it correct to think of our Lord as being conscious of his present Messiahship *before* his Resurrection.

"The historical Jesus laid claim to Messiahship only from the moment of the Resurrection." (M. 210.)

49

And a little later,

"As a matter of fact the early Synoptic tradition and the view of the primitive Church agree together completely. Both affirm with one voice that Jesus' messianic consciousness was futuristic." (M. 211.)

18. *Interims-ethik.*

"Interims-ethik" is a hybrid word which first came into use through Dr. Schweitzer, who has made the history of Ethics his own in Part II of his *Philosophy of Civilization.* He employed the word to expound the ethical thought of Jesus chiefly in the Sermon on the Mount. The word actually means 'moral behaviour for the time being.' In the case of Jesus 'the time being' means the interval between the date the words were spoken by Him and the final metamorphosis or 'New Age' of humanity which He expected would happen almost immediately, at latest within the lifetime of many who were then on earth.

Clearly enough a person's behaviour, if he were sure the world would come to an end almost at once by some catastrophic intervention and was certainly going to do so within the lifetime of many, would be likely to be very different from what that behaviour would be if there were no reason for any such expectation. Perhaps the best instance to take is the verse in the Sermon on the Mount, "Resist not evil" (Matthew v. 39). Do we accept it? Rarely indeed, and for most of us with the utmost reluctance even as individuals. As a community, never. If one reflects one finds that our Christian ministers never accept this ethic of Jesus, where the *community* is concerned. Did we resist Hitlerism? Of course we did and except by an extreme type of pacifist such resistance is approved by us all. But how comes it that we so flatly refuse to follow Jesus here? For one clear reason, that we do not accept His premises. They were in error. Jesus taught His disciples that the world was coming to an end almost at once. Had that premise been right His ethical advice would have been right. Thus Schweitzer:

"It was the same with regard to the State. The question which was put to him in the Jerusalem days had for him no practical importance. As he replied to the Pharisees' question, whether one should give tribute to Cæsar, he had no thought of defining his attitude towards the State or determining that of his followers. How could any one be concerned at all about such things! The State was simply earthly, therefore ungodly, domination. Its duration extended, therefore, only to the dawn of God's dominion. As this was near at hand, what need had one to decide if one would be tributary to the world-power or no? One might as well submit to it, its end was in fact near. Give to Cæsar what is Cæsar's and to God what is God's (Mark xii. 17)— this word is uttered with a sovereign irony against the Pharisees, who understood so little the signs of the time that this still appeared to them a question of importance. They are just as foolish in the matter of the Kingdom of God as the Sadducees with their catch-question to which husband the seven times married wife should belong at the resurrection; for they, too, leave one thing out of account —the power of God (Mark xii. 24)." (M. 119–120.)

And again:

"What do the farfetched Sadduceean arguments amount to against the possibility of the resurrection of the dead? Soon with the advent of the Kingdom, all earthly rule is done away, as well as the earthly human nature itself (M. 269.)

And with respect to the Sermon on the Mount:

"As repentance unto the Kingdom of God the ethics also of the Sermon on the Mount is interim-ethics. In this we perceive that the moral instruction of Jesus remained the same from the first day of his public appearance until his latest utterances, for the lowliness and serviceableness which he recommended to his Disciples on the way to Jerusalem correspond exactly to the new moral conduct which he developed in the Sermon on the Mount: they make one meet for the Kingdom of God." (M. 97.)

But where the Christian Church and its leaders cannot stand up to criticism is that they pretend they are following our Lord while ignoring His "Resist not evil." Yet they do not dare to admit that Jesus was certain (though wrongly so) that the world was about to come to a catastrophical end.

19. The Feeding of the Multitude.

We have in St. Mark's Gospel accounts of two such feedings, represented as miraculous, of five thousand and of four thousand. Dr. Schweitzer, in contrast with practically all other writers, claims to shew that we are hearing the account not of a miracle but of a "Solemn cultus-meal" closely resembling the Last Supper. Of this there can of course be no proof, but it is a guess of genius. As with the Last Supper we are reading of an evening meal but here the food designed for Jesus and for His disciples was, Schweitzer believes, solemnly distributed to the people and the miraculous character was ascribed by a later age. From Mark vi. 52, and viii. 14, 21, it appears that the Disciples understood nothing.

"He celebrated, therefore, a sacred cultus-meal the meaning of which was clear to Him alone. He did not count it necessary to explain to them the meaning of the ceremony." (M. 171–2.)

The recipient does not understand the significance of Jesus' action, nor does he need to do so. Without knowing it he had entered upon this table-fellowship with the Son of Man.

"The memory, however, of that mysterious supper on the lonely seashore lived on vividly in the tradition and grew to the account of the miraculous feeding. Wherein did the solemnity of this distribution consist for Jesus? The gathering at the feast is of an eschatological character. The people that gathered about Him by the seaside were awaiting with him the dawn of the Kingdom. In replacing now the customary full meal with a sacred ceremonial meal, at which he distributed food with thanksgiving to God, he acted at the prompting of his Messianic consciousness. *As one who knew himself to be the Messiah, and would be manifested to them as such at the imminent dawn of the Kingdom, he distributes, to those whom he expects soon to join him at the Messianic banquet, sacred food, as though he would give them therewith an earnest of their participation in that future solemnity."* (M. 172.)

It was a veiled eschatological Sacrament, a sacrament of salvation.

20. Why Jesus left Galilee for Jerusalem, and His reception at his Entry.

Thus does Schweitzer picture the mind of Jesus before the final journey:

"For the realisation of the Kingdom there remained but one way still open to him,—namely, conflict with the power which opposed his work. He resolved to carry this conflict into the Capital itself. There fate should decide. Perhaps the victory would fall to him. But, even if it should turn out that in the course of earthly events the fate of death awaited him inevitably, so long as he trod the path which his office prescribed, this very suffering of death must signify in God's plan the performance by which his work was to be crowned. It was then God's will that the moral state appropriate to the Kingdom of God should be inaugurated by the highest moral deed of the Messiah. With this thought he set out for Jerusalem—in order to remain Messiah." (M. 62–3.)

And in *The Quest*:

"Towards Passover, therefore, Jesus sets out for Jerusalem, solely in order to die there. 'It is,' says Wrede, 'beyond question the opinion of Mark that Jesus went to Jerusalem because He had decided to die; that is obvious even from the details of the story.' It is therefore a mistake to speak of Jesus as 'teaching' in Jerusalem. He has no intention of doing so. As a prophet He foretells in veiled parabolic form the offence which must come (Mark xii. 1–12), exhorts men to watch for the Parousia, pictures the nature of the judgment which the Son of Man shall hold, and, for the rest, thinks only how He can so provoke the Pharisees and the rulers that they will be compelled to get rid of Him. That is why He violently cleanses the Temple, and attacks the Pharisees, in the presence of the people, with passionate invective." (Q. 389.)

And of his reception by fellow-travellers on His way to the capital, and when arriving in Jerusalem, Schweitzer writes:

"Decisive is the reception which the Passover caravan accorded to Jesus as he overtook it at Jericho. This ovation was not accorded to the man who had lost ground before the Pharisees in his own country and among his own people and at last had been forced to flee, but to the celebrated prophet emerging from his retirement. If this Galilean populace supported him now by their acclaim and enabled him to terrorise the magistrates in the capital for several days—for his purification of the Temple was nothing else but that—and to expose the scribes with his dry irony, is it possible that they did it for the man who a few weeks before had to yield to these theologians in his own land?" (M. 68.)

Schweitzer holds that for Jesus this was a period of triumph.

With the feeding of the multitude Schweitzer connects that immemorial second meal.

"In this connection there falls a light upon the nature of the Last Supper at Jerusalem. There the Disciples represented the community of believers in the Kingdom. In the course of that last meal Jesus distributed to them with a word of thanksgiving food and drink. But now they know what he assumes to be: he had disclosed to them the secret of his messiahship. From this they are able to divine in his distribution the reference to the Messianic banquet. He himself gave this significance to his action in the fact that he concluded the ceremony with a hint of their proximate reunion when he should drink the wine new with them in his Father's Kingdom!" (M. 173.)

And Schweitzer continues:

"In the neighbourhood of death Jesus draws himself up to the same triumphant stature as in the days by the seaside, —for with death comes the Kingdom. On that occasion he had celebrated with the believers a mystic feast as an anticipation of the Messianic banquet; so now he rises at the end of the last earthly supper and distributes to the Disciples hallowed food and drink, intimating to them with a solemn voice that this is the last earthly meal for they are soon to be united at the banquet in the Father's Kingdom. Two corresponding parables suggest the secret of the Passion. For him, the bread and wine which he hands them at the Supper are his body and his blood, for by the sacrifice of himself unto death he ushers in the Messianic feast. The parabolic saying remained obscure to the Disciples. It was also not intended for them, its purpose was not to explain anything to them—*for it was an enigma-parable.*" (M. 271.)

Speaking both of the meal by the lake and of the meal in the upper room, Schweitzer points out how shot through and through with the idea of the sacred feast is all apocalyptic literature.

"The thought of the Messianic feast is found in Isaiah iv. 1 ff. and LXV. 12 ff. It is very strongly marked in Isaiah xxv. 6–8, a passage which perhaps dates from the time of Alexander the Great, 'and Jahweh of Hosts will prepare upon this mountain for all peoples a feast of fat things, a feast of wine on the lees, of fat things prepared with marrow, of wine on the lees well refined. He shall destroy, in this mountain, among all peoples, the veil which has veiled all peoples and the covering which has covered all nations. He shall destroy death for ever, and the Lord Jahweh shall wipe away the tears from off all faces; and the reproach of His people shall disappear from the earth." (Q. 377.) (The German follows Kautzsch's translation.)

"In Enoch xxiv. and xxv. the conception of the Messianic feast is connected with that of the tree of life which shall offer its fruits to the elect upon the mountain of the King. Similarly in the Testament of Levi, cap. xviii. 11.

"The decisive passage is in Enoch LXii. 14. After the Parousia of the Son of Man, and after the Judgment, the elect who have been saved 'shall eat with the Son of Man, shall sit down and rise up with Him to all eternity.'

"Jesus' references to the Messianic feast are therefore not merely images, but point to a reality. In Matthew viii. 11 and 12 He prophesies that many shall come from the East and from the West to sit at meat with Abraham, Isaac, and

Jacob. In Matthew xxii. 1–14 the Messianic feast is pictured as a royal marriage, in Matthew xxv. 1–13 as a marriage feast.

"The Apocalypse is dominated by the thought of the feast in all its forms. In Revelation ii. 7 it appears in connexion with the thought of the tree of life; in ii. 17 it is pictured as a feeding with manna; in iii. 21 it is the feast which the Lord will celebrate with His followers; in vii. 16, 17 there is an allusion to the Lamb who shall feed His own so that they shall no more hunger or thirst; chapter xix. describes the marriage feast of the Lamb.

"The Messianic feast therefore played a dominant part in the conception of blessedness from Enoch to the Apocalypse of John. From this we can estimate what sacramental significance a guarantee of taking part in that feast must have had. The meaning of the celebration was obvious in itself, and was made manifest in the conduct of it. The sacramental effect was wholly independent of the apprehension of the recipient. Therefore, in this also the meal at the lake-side was a true sacrament." (Q. 377–8.)

"The essential character of this historic Last Supper, as well as of the meal by the Lake of Gennesareth, consisted in its being a meal accompanied by thanksgiving which pointed forward to the Messianic feast, and at which Jesus distributed to those present food and drink. What it is possible to repeat in this action is not the distribution of food and wine by Jesus, the significance of which is dependent on its being done by Himself, but only the thanksgiving for the prospect of the Kingdom and the Messianic feast. The Early Church therefore repeated the Last Supper of Jesus with His disciples as a meal accompanied by thanksgiving which pointed forward to the Messianic feast. The reason for the repetition was the eschatological saying at the end about drinking wine new with His disciples in His Father's Kingdom. This became for the disciples a command to repeat the meal." (MP. 244.)

And again,

"We have asked, What did the disciples do between Easter and Pentecost? The answer is that day by day they waited with the other believers, holding with them the thanksgiving meal in the very room where Jesus had held the Last Supper with the disciples, expecting that the risen Jesus would return to them and, as Messiah, take His place at the feast." (MP. 252.)

22. The Passion of Jesus. The "Suffering Servant" of Isaiah.

Dr. Schweitzer teaches that it is totally wrong to imagine that when Jesus spoke of persecutions which his disciples would encounter he meant to predict what they would have to go through *after* his death; for he was sure that he would be the Messiah and that the glory of the Kingdom would then dawn. At first He thought that the great affliction would appear when he sent them out on their last mission in Matthew x. 23. But this did not take place: the disciples returned without the appearance of the Kingdom.

"But now God does not bring the Affliction to pass. And yet the atonement must be made. Then it occurred to Jesus that he as the coming Son of Man must accomplish the atonement in his own person." (м. 235.)

He then felt assured that God was sparing *them* the final sufferings and that He Himself was to bear in Himself all the Affliction, since He was the Suffering Servant foretold in Isaiah (Isaiah 42, ff.).

"From the beginning he knew himself as Messiah only in so far as he was resolved through suffering to be purified unto perfection. As the one who is destined to bear rule in the new age he must beforehand be delivered into the power of ungodliness in order that he may there approve himself for the divine lordship he is to exercise. Out of such a Messianic consciousness as this he adjures those about him to remain true so that he can recognise them as his own when the glory dawns. Thus the active ethical trait which constituted the depth of the secret of the Kingdom is a controlling factor also in the secret of Messiahship." (м. 224–5.)

And further:

"For it was no longer a question simply of the suffering which the great herald of the Kingdom must undergo in company with His own in the final Affliction; but now He suffers who is to be the Messiah. This suffering, moreover, does not any longer occur in the general Affliction of the last times, but Jesus suffers alone, and His suffering is now represented as a purely earthly, historical event!" (м. 225.)

And again:

"With the revelation at Cæsarea Philippi cease all intimations that the believers must pass with Jesus through the Affliction. According to the secret which He imparts to the Disciples He alone suffers." (м. 230–1.)

60

Moreover, Schweitzer regards Jesus as seeing Himself to be Isaiah's Suffering Servant (Isaiah xl. 1–11, xlii. 1, lii. 1, and liii.).

"Isaiah 40 to 66 was nothing else but the prophetic representation of the events of the last time in the midst of which he knew himself to be.

"The passage commences with the proclamation that God's reign is about to begin. The preparer of the way comes upon the scene. He cries that the earthly passes away when the Lord, dealing reward and recompense, appears in his glory. The hour dawns in which he gathers his flock and brings in the era of peace.

"The Elect is there. He proclaims righteousness in truth. God has put his spirit upon him (Isaiah xlii. 1 ff.). He shall establish judgment upon the earth; the cities wait upon his teaching. But before the glory dawns and the bearer of the divine spirit rules with power and righteousness over the peoples He must pass through an estate of humiliation. Others do not understand why He is put to shame. They think God has rejected Him, and know not that He bears their infirmities, is pierced for their transgressions, and smitten for their offences. The oppressed servant is meek and openeth not his mouth. For the transgression of the people He is stricken to death. Then, however, will the Lord glorify Him. He hath called Him to this from His mother's womb. He is ordained to bring again Jacob and to save Israel. He shall be for a light to the Gentiles, that God's salvation may extend unto the ends of the earth (Isaiah, xlix. 1 ff.; lii. 1 ff.; liii. 1 ff.)." (M. 236–7.)

And once more:

"Jesus' idea of the Passion is in the end completely absorbed in that of the Deutero-Isaiah. Like the servant of God, He too is destined to reign in glory. But first He appears, meek and unrecognised, in the role of a preacher who works righteousness. He must pass also through suffering and humiliation ere God permits the glorious consummation to dawn. What He endures is an atonement for the iniquity of others. This is a secret between Himself and God." (M. 238.)

Concerning the Entry into Jerusalem Schweitzer writes:

"Jesus Himself made the preparations for the Messianic entry. Its Messianic features were due to His arrangements. He made a point of riding upon the ass, not because He was weary, but because He desired that the Messianic prophecy of Zechariah ix. 9 should be secretly fulfilled." (Q. 391.)

"Jesus therefore made His entry into Jerusalem as the Prophet, as Elias." (Q. 392.)

And thus Dr. Schweitzer understands Gethsemane: He prays for Deliverance, he prays for His three disciples:

"There is a quality of compassionate consideration for others in the thought that He makes satisfaction in the Passion for the adherents of the Kingdom, in order that they may be exempted from the trial in which perchance they might prove weak. The petition, 'Lead us not into Temptation, but deliver us from the Evil,' is now fulfilled in His passion.

"This deeply human trait is especially evident in Gethsemane. Only over the three intimate Disciples still hovers the possibility that they may be obliged to pass with Him through suffering and temptation. The sons of Zebedee, to secure their claim to sit with Him upon the throne, boasted that they could drink with Him His cup and undergo with

Him the baptism of suffering—and this prospect He held out to them (Mark x. 38, 40). Peter, however, swore that he would not deny Him; even if all others should forsake Him, he desired to die with Him (Mark xiv. 31). These three Jesus had taken with Him to the place where He prayed. While He implored God that the cup might pass Him by, there overcame Him a sorrowful anxiety for the Three. If God does not actually send them with Him through the Passion, will they hold out as they are bold to believe? Wherefore He is mindful of them in that sad hour. Twice He arouses Himself and wakes them out of sleep, bidding them watch and pray to God that He lead them not into the Temptation, even if God will not spare Him this cup; for the spirit is willing, but the flesh is weak. That is perhaps the most touching moment in Jesus' life. Some have dared to call Gethsemane Jesus' weak hour; but in reality it is precisely the hour in which His supernatural greatness is revealed in His deeply human compassion." (M. 240.)

And at last He prays for Himself:

". . . it is once more made clear that for Jesus the necessity of His death is grounded in dogma, not in external historical facts. Above the dogmatic eschatological necessity, however, there stands the omnipotence of God, which is bound by no limitations. As Jesus in the Lord's Prayer had taught His followers to pray for deliverance from the πειρασμος, and as in His fears for the Three He bids them pray for the same thing, so now He Himself prays for deliverance, even in this last moment when He knows that the armed band which is coming to arrest Him is already on the way. Literal history does not exist for Him, only the will of God; and this is exalted even above eschatological necessity." (Q. 390.)

23. His Trial and His Betrayal by Judas.

How came Caiaphas at our Lord's trial to be in possession
of proof by which Jesus could be and was condemned to
death for blasphemy? Here Dr. Schweitzer once again offers a guess of genius.

"He was arrested and condemned on account of His Messianic claims. But how did the High Priest know that Jesus
claimed to be the Messiah? And why does he put the ac-
cusation as a direct question without calling witnesses in
support of it? Why was the attempt first made to bring up
a saying about the Temple which could be interpreted as
blasphemy in order to condemn Him on this ground (Mark
xiv. 57–59)? Before that again, as is evident from Mark's
account, they had brought up a whole crowd of witnesses
in the hope of securing sufficient evidence to justify His
condemnation; and the attempt had not succeeded." (Q.
391.)

The entry into Jerusalem had not been a Messianic ovation:

"Except Jesus and the disciples, therefore, no one knew
the secret of His Messiahship even in those days at Jerusalem. But the High Priest suddenly showed himself in possession of it. How? Through the betrayal of Judas.

"The traitorous act of Judas cannot have consisted in in-
forming the Sanhedrin where Jesus could be found at a
suitable place for an arrest. They could have had that information more cheaply by causing Jesus to be watched by
spies. But Mark expressly says that Judas when he betrayed
Jesus did not yet know of a favourable opportunity for the

arrest, but was seeking such an opportunity. Mark xiv. 10, 11, 'And Judas Iscariot, one of the twelve, went unto the chief priests, to betray him unto them. And when they heard it, they were glad, and promised to give him money. And he sought how he might conveniently betray him.'

"The betrayal by which he brought his Master to death, in consequence of which the rulers decided upon the arrest, knowing that their cause was safe in any case, was the betrayal of the Messianic secret. Jesus died because two of His disciples had broken His command of silence: Peter when He made known the secret of the Messiahship to the Twelve at Cæsarea Philippi; Judas Iscariot by communicating it to the High Priest. But the difficulty was that Judas was the sole witness. Therefore the betrayal was useless so far as the actual trial was concerned unless Jesus admitted the charge. So they first tried to secure His condemnation on other grounds, and only when these attempts broke down did the High Priest put, in the form of a question, the charge in support of which he could have brought no witnesses." (Q. 394.)

"But Jesus immediately admitted it, and strengthened the admission by an allusion to His Parousia in the near future as Son of Man." (Q. 395.)

And how are we to account for the cries of "Crucify Him: Crucify Him" uttered by a mob which four days before welcomed Him with such enthusiasm at His Entry into Jerusalem?

"The priests went among the people and induced them not to agree to the Procurator's proposal. How? By telling them why He was condemned, by revealing to them the

Messianic secret. That makes Him at once from a prophet worthy of honour into a deluded enthusiast and blasphemer. That was the explanation of the "fickleness" of the Jerusalem mob which is always so eloquently described, without any evidence for it except this single inexplicable case." (Q. 395.)

And thus in *The Mystery of the Kingdom of God:*

"They got the decisive charge through the betrayed secret of Cæsarea Philippi. To be Elijah, the prophet of the last times, was no religious crime. But to claim to be the Messiah, that was blasphemy! The perfidy of the charge lay in the High Priest's insinuation that Jesus held himself to be the Messiah, just as he stood there before him. This Jesus repudiated with a proud word about his coming as Son of Man. Nevertheless he was condemned for blasphemy." (M. 217.)

But the admission by the accused, so cunningly obtained by the Chief Priest through the betrayal of Jesus by Judas, is instantly followed by the full eschatological assertion of Jesus.

"After Jesus with his 'Yes' had Himself pronounced the verdict of death He speaks of His 'coming again' upon the clouds of heaven. Hereby, according to Mark's text, He associates the two events in a single thought. Mark xiv. 62: I am, and ye shall see the Son of Man sitting at the right hand of the Power and coming with the clouds of Heaven." (M. 78.)

In like manner at the Transfiguration He foretold the almost immediate end of the world and the coming of the New Age. Mark viii. 38.

24. Dr. Schweitzer's last words in "The Quest."

"He comes to us as One unknown, without a name, as of old, by the lake-side, He came to those men who knew Him not. He speaks to us the same word: 'Follow thou me!' and sets us to the tasks which He has to fulfil for our time. He commands. And to those who obey Him, whether they be wise or simple, He will reveal Himself in the toils, the conflicts, the sufferings which they shall pass through in His Fellowship, and, as an ineffable mystery, they shall learn in their own experience Who He is." (Q. 401.)

APPENDICES

I. Baptism an Eschatological Sacrament.

"In the Pauline theology very striking prominence is given to the thought of being sealed unto salvation. The apostle is conscious of bearing about with him in his body 'the marks of Jesus' (Galatians vi. 17), the 'dying' of Jesus (2 Corinthians iv. 10). This sign is received in baptism, since it is a baptism 'into the death of Christ'; in this act the recipient is in a certain sense really buried with Him, and thenceforth walks among men as one who belongs, even here below, to risen humanity (Romans vi. 1 ff.). Baptism is the seal, the earnest of the spirit, the pledge of that which is to come (2 Corinthians i. 22; Ephesians i. 13, 14, iv. 30).

"This conception of baptism as a 'salvation' in view of that which was to come goes down through the whole of ancient theology. Its preaching might really be summed up in the words, 'Keep your baptism holy and without blemish.'" (Q. 375.)

"In the Apocalypse of John the thought of the sealing stands prominently in the foreground. The locusts receive power to hurt those only who have not the seal of God on their foreheads (Revelation ix. 4, 5). The beast (Revelation xiii. 16 ff.) compels men to bear his mark; only those who will not accept it are to reign with Christ (Revelation xx. 4). The chosen hundred and forty-four thousand bear the name

68

of God and the name of the Lamb upon their foreheads (Revelation xiv. 1).

"It is a mistake to regard baptism with water as a 'symbolic act' in the modern sense, and make the Baptist decry his own wares by saying, 'I baptize only with water, but the other can baptize with the Holy Spirit.'" (Q. 376.)

"The baptism of John was therefore an eschatological sacrament pointing forward to the pouring forth of the spirit and to the judgment, a provision for 'salvation.' Hence the wrath of the Baptist when he saw Pharisees and Sadducees crowding to his baptism: 'Ye generation of vipers, who hath warned you to flee from the wrath to come? Bring forth now fruits meet for repentance.' (Matthew iii. 7, 8). By the reception of baptism, that is, they are saved from the judgment." (Q. 377.)

". . . . . we may think of Baptism and the Lord's Supper as from the first eschatological sacraments in the eschatological movement which later detached itself from Judaism under the name of Christianity. That explains why we find them both in Paul and in the earliest theology as sacramental acts, not as symbolic ceremonies, and find them dominating the whole Christian doctrine." (Q. 378.)

". . . . . the adoption of the baptism of John in Christian practice cannot be explained except on the assumption that it was the sacrament of the eschatological community, a revealed means of securing 'salvation' which was not altered in the slightest by the Messiahship of Jesus. How else could we explain the fact that baptism, without any commandment of Jesus, and without Jesus ever having baptized, was taken over, as a matter of course, into Christianity, and was given a special reference to the receiving of the Spirit?" (Q. 378–9.)

"If Christianity as the religion of historically revealed mysteries was able to lay hold upon Hellenism and overcome it, the reason of this was that it was already in its purely eschatological beginnings a religion of sacraments, a religion of eschatological sacraments, since Jesus had recognized a Divine institution in the baptism of John, and had Himself performed a sacramental action in the distribution of food at the Lake of Gennesareth and at the Last Supper." (Q. 379.)

The foregoing passages from *The Quest* triumphantly established Schweitzer's teaching concerning baptism in the time of Jesus.

II. *The Eschatology of the Lord's Prayer.*

Thus does Dr. Schweitzer write in *The Mystery of the Kingdom of God* of the Lord's Prayer:

". . . . . the Affliction also of the last times had its place indeed in the divinely ordained course of the Messianic drama. But yet it lay in God's unrestricted omnipotence that He might eliminate it and permit the Kingdom to dawn without this season of trial. Therefore men might pray God that He would suffer that heavy hour of probation to pass by. Jesus enjoined this upon His Disciples in the same prayer in which He taught them to make petition for the coming Kingdom. He teaches them to implore God for the final state of blessedness, in which His name will be hallowed and His will be done on earth as it is in heaven; but at the same time they are to beg Him not to lead them into the 'Temptation,' not to give them into the power of the Evil, not to oblige them to make satisfaction for their sins by the endurance of the Affliction of the last times; but to deliver them by His omnipotence from the power of the evil when the ungodly world for the last time asserts itself at the coming of the Kingdom for which they pray. That is the inner connection of the last three petitions of the Lord's Prayer.

"The Lord's Prayer thus exhibits in the first three and the last three petitions a purely eschatological character. We have the same contrast as in the Beatitudes, the charge to the Apostles, the embassage to the Baptist, and the discourse at Bethsaida. First it is a question of the coming of the Affliction of the last times. We perceive from the Lord's Prayer, however, that there is no absolute necessity for this Affliction, but that it is only relatively determined in God's almighty will." (M. 228–9.)

"The Affliction, in fact, represents in its extremest form the repentance requisite for the Kingdom. Whosoever comes through that test approved makes satisfaction for his transgressions in the godless æon. Through conflict and suffering men wrest themselves free from this power to become instruments of the divine will in the Kingdom of God. That is to be conceived collectively. The faithful adherents of the Kingdom as a community make the satisfaction. The individual thereby perfects and approves himself. Such is God's will. Jesus, however, prays with them to God that He may be pleased in His omnipotence to forgive them the debt without satisfaction, as they forgive their debtors. That means remission pure and simple, without atonement. May it please God not to lead them through the 'Temptation,' but straightway to release them from the power of the world.

"Only so can one understand how Jesus throughout His

ministry can assume forgiveness of sins and yet here expressly prays for it; and how He can speak of a temptation which comes from God. It is a question in fact of the general Messianic remission of debts and the Temptation of the Messianic Affliction. Therefore these petitions constitute the conclusion of the Kingdom-prayer." (M. 229–30.)

And lastly:

"The conception of the Messianic feast finds a place also in the Lord's Prayer, for in the fourth petition the correct translation refers not only to daily bread but to the Messianic Feast." (MP. 239.)

III. Did Jesus Mean to Found a Church?

"Jesus promises them expressly that at the appearing of the Son of Man they shall sit upon twelve thrones, judging the twelve tribes of Israel (Matthew xix. 28). It is to their part in the judgment that belongs also the authority to bind and to loose which He entrusts to them—first to Peter personally (Matthew xvi. 19) and afterwards to all the Twelve (Matthew xviii. 18)—in such a way, too, that their present decisions will be somehow or other binding at the Judgment. Or does the 'upon earth' refer only to the fact that the Messianic Last Judgment will be held on earth? 'I give unto thee the Keys of the Kingdom of Heaven, and whatsoever thou shalt bind on earth shall be bound in heaven, and whatsoever thou shalt loose on earth shall be loosed in heaven' (Matthew xvi. 19.) Why should these words not be historical? Is it because in the same context Jesus speaks of the 'church' which He will found upon the Rock-disciple? But if one has once got a clear idea from Paul, 2 Clement, the Epistle to the Hebrews, and the Shepherd of Hermas, what the preexisting 'church' was which was to appear in the last times, it will no longer appear impossible that Jesus might have spoken of the church against which the gates of hell shall not prevail. Of course, if the passage is given an uneschatological reference to the Church as we know it, it loses all real meaning and becomes a treasure-trove to the Roman Catholic exegete, and a terror to the Protestant." (Q. 369.)

From this footnote on p. 369 of *The Quest* Dr. Schweitzer shews clearly that he holds the famous passage Matthew xvi. 19 to be solely an eschatological pronouncement of our Lord and that in no way had He in mind a mundane church continuing from century to century. How indeed could that be in the mind of Jesus since three times (Matthew x. 23; Mark ix. 1, and xiii. 30) He foretold the catastrophical coming of the Kingdom in the lifetime of many then alive, and on a final occasion told Caiaphas that he also would see the end of the present world and the Last Judgment?

IV. *The Little Apocalypse.*

(Mark XIII, especially vv. 24–30.)

This notable passage in the New Testament so strongly supports Dr. Schweitzer's main contention, that Jesus was certain that the world was about to come to an end, that one is surprised at meeting the following passage in the "Mystery":

"Even though Mark XIII may contain single eschatological sayings attributable to Jesus, the discourse as such is necessarily unhistorical. It betrays the perspective of the time after Jesus' death. During the days at Jerusalem Jesus could speak of no general Affliction before the coming of the Son of Man. The Synoptic apocalypse stands in direct contradiction to the secret of the Passion, since this indeed simply abolishes the general Affliction of the last times. Therefore it is unhistorical. Apocalyptic discourses with intimation of the final Affliction belong to the Galilean period at the time of the mission of the Twelve. The discourse to the Apostles on that occasion is the historical Synoptic apocalypse. About a time of Affliction after his death Jesus never uttered a word to His Disciples, for it lay beyond his field of vision." (M. 246–7.)

But the fact that Schweitzer agrees that the passage may be based on words of Our Lord at the time of the sending out of the Twelve apostles (Matthew x, 1–23) and that similar apocalyptic discourses, dated in the Galilean period, are *the* historical synoptic apocalypse would seem to entitle the reader to connect closely these verses (especially xiii, 30) with the teaching of Jesus.

That Dr. Schweitzer is of such a mind is clear from the following passage from pp. 78–79 of *The Mystery*.

"A close connection between the thought of the Passion and eschatology is implied also in Jesus' saying about the path of suffering which his followers must tread (Mk. 8. 34 to 9–1.) Whosoever shall be ashamed of Jesus when he suffers reproach and persecution in this adulterous and sinful world, of him will the Son of Man be ashamed when he cometh in the glory of His Father with the holy angels. For

74

this generation shall not sink into the grave until they see the Kingdom of God come with power!" (м. 78–9.)

V. Pauline Eschatology.

". . . . . our only information about the beliefs of the primitive Church comes from Paul. His writings are the first —and indeed the only—witnesses which we possess upon the point, since the First Epistle of Peter and the Epistle of James give us information at best about a non-Pauline, certainly not about a pre-Pauline Christianity."

Dr. Schweitzer is one of the most learned students of St. Paul in the history of Christian thought. In this Part are offered to the reader excerpts from his two classic works, *Paul and His Interpreters* (1912) and *The Mysticism of Paul the Apostle* (1931).

"The Pauline Christ, even though He is called the Son of God, is not God, but only a heavenly Being. The renewal which is effected by fellowship with Him is not a deification —the word never occurs in the Apostle's writings—but only a transference into a state of super-sensuous corporeity, which has to do with a coming new condition of the world." (p. 223.)

". . . . . the study of Late Judaism had been going its own way. The further it advanced the more evident it became that this was the soil on which the theology of Paul had grown up."

"The eschatology of Paul is therefore quite different from

75

that of Jesus, a fact which has been hitherto never duly appreciated. Instead of thinking as Jesus did along the lines of the simple eschatology of the Books of Daniel and Enoch, he represents the two-fold eschatology of the Scribes.

"It is probably connected with the eschatological view of the circles from which he came that Paul never uses the expression 'Son of Man.' This is absent from the Apocalypse of Baruch also. Nevertheless he thinks of the Messiah as the Son-of-Man Messiah, because he represents Him as appearing upon the clouds of heaven." (MP. 90.)

Chapter VI. of *The Mysticism of Paul* concerns the Mystical Doctrine of the Dying and Rising again with Christ. Essentially relevant to this is the following from that volume:

"What, then, was the origin of this Christ-Mysticism which flashes up like a will-o'-the-wisp in disconnected sayings? In the main it goes back to the vision on the Damascus road. Everything which can be called Christ-Mysticism in Paul comes from his reaction to this initiatory experience." In the Damascus experience Paul attained to the conviction not only that Jesus was the expected Messiah but also to the 'in Christ' and 'Christ in me.' His Christ-Mysticism is only the radiation of the energy which thenceforth was concentrated in his soul." (MP. 35.)

And thus does Schweitzer outline Paul's eschatological thought:

"According to the eschatological doctrine the Elect are saved because by the death and resurrection of Jesus Christ the end of the dominion of the angelic powers, and therewith the end of the natural world, is brought about. It is therefore certain that He will soon appear in His glory and open the way for His Elect, whether they be already dead or still living, to enter the Messianic glory." (MP. 25.)

And again:

"Pauline mysticism is concerned with the passing away and restoration of the world, and the fate of the Elect amid these events. It does not even assume that all will die, but expects that many of them will live to see the end of the world while still in their mortal bodies, and will enter, transformed, into the glory to which they have become entitled through the being-in-Christ.

"The fact that it occurs in connection with the expectation of the end of the world, and is founded upon cosmic events, gives its distinctive character to the Pauline mysticism." (MP. 23.)

But in no other book will be found more precisely delineated and with clearer and more unavoidable texts the whole Pauline eschatology:

"From his first letter to his last Paul's thought is always uniformly dominated by the expectation of the immediate return of Jesus, of the judgment, and the Messianic glory.

"In the first Thessalonian Epistle sayings constantly occur which give expression to this ardent expectation.

"I Thessalonians i. 10: 'To await the Coming from heaven of His Son Whom He raised from the dead, Jesus, Who has delivered us from the Wrath which is on its way.'

"I Thessalonians ii. 19: 'For who is our hope, our joy, our crown if it be not you (to present you) before the face of our Lord Jesus Christ at His appearing.'

"I Thessalonians iii. 13: 'To confirm your hearts that they may be blameless in holiness before God our Father at the appearing of the Lord Jesus Christ with His saints.'

77

"I Thessalonians v. 23: 'May He, the God of Peace, make you holy through and through, and keep you, spirit, soul and body complete, blameless at the appearing of Our Lord Jesus Christ.'

"The Letters to the Galatians, Corinthians, and Romans are in the main so occupied with arguments about the Law, righteousness of faith, being-in-Christ, predestination, and the particular affairs of the churches, that it is possible to forget the expectation which dominates the soul of the writer. But suddenly, in some incidental saying, the eschatological belief stands there in all its strength as something which always underlies the whole.

"Galatians i. 4: 'Jesus Who gave Himself for our sins that He might pluck us forth from this present evil world.'

"Galatians vi. 10: 'Therefore, so long as we have time, let us do good . . . . .'" (MP. 52.)

"In the 1st Epistle to the Corinthians the convictions about marrying and remaining single are dominated by the conviction that the time is short (I Corinthians vii. 22) and that 'the fashion of this world is passing away' (I Corinthians vii. 31). Believers are reminded that they are the generation 'That will outlive the end of time' (I Corinthians x. 11), and that in the time to come they will pronounce judgment upon angels (I Corinthians vi. 3), that they themselves must be present at a judgment in which all things shall be tested by fire (I Corinthians iii. 13–15), and that the celebration of the Lord's Supper is a remembering of the death of Jesus which looks to His coming again (I Corinthians xi. 26). At the beginning of the Letter there is a reference to the revelation of the glory of Christ (I Corinthians i. 7–8) and it closes with the exclamatory prayer *Maramatha* ('Our Lord, Come!', I Corinthians xvi. 22).

"In 2nd Corinthians also there is frequent reference to the expectation of the day of the Lord.

"II Corinthians i. 14: 'That we are your boasting, as you also are ours in the day of Our Lord Jesus.'

"II Corinthians v. 10: 'For we all must be made manifest before the judgment seat of Christ.'

"II Corinthians xi. 2: 'For I have betrothed you to a husband, to present you as a pure virgin to Christ.'

"Imposing expressions of this eschatological expectation are found also in the Epistle to the Romans. The Apostle represents the whole creation as yearning for the day of the revelation of the sons of God (I Romans viii. 19). He holds that Redemption is nearer now than at the time when he and the Roman Christians first believed (Romans xiii. 11), that the morning of the expected day is already beginning to dawn (Romans xiii. 12), and that God will shortly tread Satan underfoot (Romans xvi. 20).

"In the Epistle to the Philippians eschatological expectation recurs again and again, as in 1st Thessalonians.

"Philippians i. 6: 'That He Who has begun in you a good work will complete it against the day of Christ.'

"Philippians, i. 10: 'That you may be pure and without offence for the day of Christ.'

"Philippians ii. 10: 'That you hold fast by the word of life, so that you may be my boast for the day of Christ.'

"Philippians iii. 20–22: 'For our home is in heaven, from whence also we expect the Lord Jesus Christ as our Deliverer, Who shall change the body of our humiliation that it may be conformed to the body of His glory.'

79

"Philippians iv. 1–5: 'Rejoice in the Lord at all times! And once more I say, rejoice! . . . . The Lord is at hand!'" (MP. 52–3.)

And finally we have Dr. Schweitzer's words illuminating the great passages in Thessalonians I:

"The destruction of the dominion of the Angels will be completed by the Return of Jesus. His appearing will not be announced by preliminary signs (I Thessalonians v. 1–4). Suddenly He is there. At His coming there will sound from heaven a voice of command; the voice of the Angel will be heard; the trumpet of God rings out. Those believers who have already 'fallen asleep' will awaken, and those who are still alive will pass through a transformation into the mode of being which belongs to the resurrection. All together will be caught up into the clouds of heaven to meet the Lord in the air, and will thenceforth abide with Him for ever (I Thessalonians iv. 16–17)." (MP. 65.)

And we may quote from *The Quest* itself:

"In seeking clues to the eschatology of Jesus, scholars have passed over the eschatology which lies closest to it, that of Paul. But why? Is it not identical with that of Jesus, at least in so far that both are 'Jewish eschatology'? Did not Reimarus long ago declare that the eschatology of the primitive Christian community was identical with the Jewish, and only went beyond it in claiming a definite knowledge on a single point which was unessential in the nature and course of the expected events, in knowing, that is, who the Son of Man should be? That Christians drew no distinction between their own eschatology and the Jewish is evident from the whole character of the earlier apocalyptic literature, and

not least from the Apocalypse of John! After all, what altera-
tion did the belief that Jesus was the Son of Man who was
to be revealed make in the general scheme of the course of
apocalyptic events?" (Q. 365.)

CONCLUSION

So ends this short account of the eschatological teaching of Dr. Albert Schweitzer, first offered to the world forty or fifty years ago. To the present writer the thoughts of Dr. Schweitzer, both in his theological and in his philosophical works, brought a meaning and value beyond all that had been offered to him before, and for this the gratitude of a lifetime is all too little.

One feels in reading *The Mystery* and *The Quest* a sense of truthfulness and of entire absence of any partisan attempt to select the facts to suit past orthodox teaching. Dr. Schweitzer's picture of Jesus and exposition of His thoughts and words are as beautiful as they appear to be true. Perhaps the strongest evidence for Schweitzer's theological position is the rarity of its public discussion by clergy. Ask, as I have done, some prominent Anglican or Free Church theologian what works to consult to supply a case *against* the last pages of *The Quest* and you will meet little more fortune than met me in my own search. I myself was offered nothing of value. Or enquire* when the B.B.C. Religious Advisory Committee has allowed discussion on the Schweitzer teaching and you may be told that such discussion has not been allowed "on the air," and if the question is pressed further you are likely to be told that silence is imposed because Schweitzer's escha-

* In March 1947 the Governors of the B.B.C. announced that af-firmations of widely differing beliefs will in future be allowed.

tology is "not in the stream of the Christian tradition." It was not in such fashion that Christianity was brought into the world. When the same Jewish Sanhedrin that had condemned Jesus to a shameful death attempted to prevent His apostles from spreading His Gospel so new to the Jews, it was Gamaliel who gave to the rulers the immortal advice:

> "And now I say unto you, Refrain from these men, and let them alone: for if this counsel or this work be of men, it will come to nought: But if it be of God, ye cannot overthrow it; lest haply ye be found even to fight against God." (Acts v. 34–39).

In this short compendium of certain Christian thought, thought unequalled in its urge since the Reformation, the present compiler has endeavoured to make Dr. Schweitzer's teaching better known, and to build upon his *ipsissima verba*. But to all Christian inquirers one would say, "Read for yourself. Read the last fifty-two pages of *The Quest* or the whole of *The Mystery of the Kingdom of God* and read also Chapter VI. and the Epilogue of Dr. Schweitzer's *My Life and Thought*."

Remember too that this very great thinker and very great Christian offers also to the world a *Philosophy of Civilisation* (two volumes have already been published, two are in process of completion) in which his ethical thought is in the end based upon that sure foundation of the human heart, "Reverence for Life."

EPILOGUE BY
ALBERT SCHWEITZER

The Conception of the Kingdom of God
in the
Transformation of Eschatology

The Conception of the Kingdom of God
in the Transformation of Eschatology

Colonel E. N. Mozley here presents the views which I have expressed, in writings on the teaching and life of Jesus, concerning the extent and nature of the influence of late Jewish eschatology upon his expectation and proclamation of the Kingdom of God, and upon the way in which he regarded himself as Messiah. A valuable service is rendered to present-day theology by this forcible reminder. The author sets himself in opposition to the prevalent tendency to overlook the meaning to Jesus of that eschatology and to evade the problem which this raises.

I welcome the invitation to write an epilogue to this book, for it gives me the opportunity to develop my ideas concerning the effect upon Christian faith of non-fulfilment, and concerning the significance of the idea of the Kingdom of God throughout Christian history and at the present time.

The primitive Christian hope of an immediate coming of the Kingdom of God was based on the teaching of Jesus; yet the fact that it remained unfulfilled did not shatter Christian faith. How was the catastrophe dealt with? What transformation of the faith enabled it to survive the surrender of the original expectation?

Although the eschatological problem has been under discussion for more than a generation, until quite recently only three factors have usually been taken into consideration as determining the development and re-shaping of Christian belief, *viz.*, the struggle for unity, the conflict with second century Gnosticism, and accommodation to Greek metaphysics. But these do not cover the whole ground. A fourth factor was at work, much more strongly than has been admitted, *viz.*, the inescapable abandonment of the early hope of a speedy coming of the Kingdom of God. The effect of this has been studied in detail for the first time by Martin Werner in *Die Entstehung des Christlichen Dogmas* (Paul Haupt, Bern, 1941).

. . . .

The apostle Paul had to wrestle with the problem, but it did not seriously affect him, because he took the view that the coming of the Kingdom was only postponed for a short time. He was thus able to hold to his conviction that the Kingdom must come as the immediate consequence of the self-sacrifice of Jesus on the Cross. His theory is that the Kingdom of God has actually come in the death and resurrection of Jesus, and is actually present, though not yet revealed. Those events inaugurated the transformation of the world of nature into the supernatural world of the Kingdom of God. Through mystical fellowship with the crucified and risen Jesus Christ, believers already share with him the supernatural quality of life in the Kingdom; they are already risen, though they look like ordinary people.

This view enables Paul to distinguish between the coming of the Kingdom and its manifestation. He regards the earlier view, with its hope fixed simply on the future, as falling short of the truth. His whole theology rests on this ante-dating, which is bound up with the assurance that Jesus himself expected the Kingdom to arrive with his resurrection as the result of his death.

The greatest thinker in the early Church thus holds both views side by side; the Kingdom is to come, and it is growing,—and the latter tends to displace the former. But the new view cannot cover the whole ground, because it starts from the theory of a brief postponement, which time will soon disprove. The early Church as a whole rejected this doctrine, holding that the death and resurrection of Jesus simply made it possible for the Kingdom to come some time, and that they must be content to wait for it.

From the second generation onwards the arrival of the Kingdom becomes "one far-off divine event," and in later days it is infinitely far away. This change of necessity affects the nature of the expectation. Originally it held a dominant position at the very centre of the faith; now it falls into the background. Instead of being the very essence of belief, it is now just one article among others.

When the Kingdom was expected immediately, it had a meaning for the present, which it overshadowed. The believer looked for a redemption which would lift him, with the multitude of his fellow-believers, into a world no longer subject to mortality and evil. With such a hope, he felt himself already delivered out of this world. But the Kingdom has no such meaning for the present, when it is imagined as being far away; the believer knows that he is condemned to live out his life in the same old world.

Denial of the world is a different thing when the end is not impending. It presented little difficulty to those for whom the other world was so near; but to those who can cherish no hope of seeing the arrival of the new world, life must mean the denial of this world from first to last. These can have no hope for the world and its inhabitants; hopelessness about the present situation goes along with belief in the coming of the Kingdom of God at the end. Moreover, the fact that the Kingdom is merely something to be waited for has an unfortunate corollary. It made no difference to those who expected it immediately; but it obviously creates an unnatural situation for those whose faith compels them to do nothing but wait for the Kingdom which comes entirely of itself. Both by their denial of the world and by their belief that the Kingdom comes of itself, they are condemned to refrain from all efforts to improve the present situation.

While Christianity has to tread this path, it cannot be to the surrounding Graeco-Roman world what it ought to be. It cannot use its moral energy as power for regenerating the empire and its peoples. It conquers paganism; it becomes the religion of the state. But owing to its peculiar character it must leave the state to its fate. This world is not the dough in which its leaven can work.

The idea of redemption was also affected by the change of outlook. Originally the dominant thought of the Kingdom of God meant that believers shared with one another the blessings of a new creation. But now the experience of the individual took precedence of that of the community. Each separate believer is now concerned with his own redemption. He cares nothing for the future of mankind and of the world. There is something cold and unnatural about the naive egoism of such piety.

The abandonment of eager expectation meant that Christianity lost the joy which characterised it in the days of Paul and the early Church. It started in bright sunshine, but had to continue its journey in the chilly gloom of a vague and uncertain hope. The idea of the Kingdom of God is no longer at the centre of faith, and this has led to a far-reaching impoverishment.

. . . .

The substitution of the distant view for the near view of the coming of the Kingdom of God necessitates the elaboration and re-shaping of the faith. Originally the believer expected to come into possession of the blessedness of redemption through immediate admission into the Kingdom opened by the death and resurrection of Jesus. But when these blessings are postponed until the end of time, demands are made of faith which cannot be met by the earlier doctrine of redemption. The old assurance of the immediate attainment of the blessedness of redemption has now faded, and must be replaced by the assurance of a right, secured by the death and resurrection of Jesus, to the blessedness of the Kingdom of God at the end of time. The early Christians thought of redemption and blessedness as different aspects of the same experience. Later they were separated in time, and each came to have its own meaning. Instead of blessedness as such, the believer had the blessedness of being assured of his right to redemption; and this gave him strength to bear the burden of life in this world.

It became necessary, in the development of the doctrine of redemption, to have a comprehensive interpretation of the death and resurrection of Jesus, showing how these guarantee future blessedness to the believer. Faith feels that it must be clear on this point. Christian theology was entirely occupied, in the first centuries, with meeting the demand of faith for a fuller understanding of the death and resurrection of Jesus.

Assurance of a share in the coming blessedness naturally depends upon the assurance of having received the forgiveness of sins and the power of the resurrection already in this present life. Resurrection and acquittal on the Day of Judgment on the ground that sins have already been forgiven: these are the conditions of entrance into the Kingdom of God and its blessedness. Christianity had been the religion of faith in the Kingdom of God; now it became the religion of faith in the resurrection and the forgiveness of sins.

Greek theology is chiefly interested in the problem of reaching certainty with regard to the possession of power to rise again from the dead; in the west it is the forgiveness of sins of which theology wants to make sure. The task was made easier in both cases by the work which Paul had done. He was the first to tackle the question of being actually redeemed before the full revelation of the Kingdom of God; and he solved it in his own way. Later generations, however, could not simply adopt his solution, since they lacked the glowing eschatological expectation which lay behind his doctrine of the possession of eternal life and the forgiveness of sins through mystical union with Christ. But Paul's theology is a magnificent structure, and it provided material which could be used for buildings of another style.

* * * *

The creators of Greek theology are known to us through their writings: Ignatius, bishop of Antioch, who suffered martyrdom in Rome in the second decade of the second century; Justin Martyr, born in Palestine, who shared the same fate in Rome in 165; and Irenaeus, from Asia Minor, who was made bishop of Lyons in 178.

Their teaching starts from Paul's view of the power of resurrection, which the Spirit imparts to the physical nature of Jesus and of believers. Appropriating this, they develop and re-shape it. Their re-shaping consists in placing the work of the Spirit, which follows upon the death and resurrection of Jesus, in the long continuing course of the natural order, whereas Paul assigned it to the era during which the natural world was being transformed into the supernatural world of the Kingdom of God.

Greek theology only found it possible to assert, as if it were quite obvious, that the Spirit prepares the body for the coming resurrection, because this was stated in Paul's epistles. There was nothing in the primitive Christian doctrine of the Spirit to justify the idea, but Paul's teaching gave it apostolic authority. His sovereign treatment of the Jewish eschatological doctrine of the work of the Spirit gave to the Christian faith something which Greek religious thought could appropriate. Ignatius, Justin and Irenaeus turned the eschatological mysticism of being "in Christ" into Greek mysticism.

The fundamental idea in Greek theology is that the Spirit first entered into union with human flesh in the person of Jesus, and thus gained the power to work upon man's physical nature. This power was further exercised among men after Jesus was separated from the world by his death and resurrection. As a new principle of life, it regenerates men spiritually and physically, so that they are fitted for eventual entrance into the Kingdom of God. The new life, which is for Paul the effect of being already risen with Christ, is regarded by Greek theology as being born again through the Spirit; the theory of dying and rising again with Christ is gone. The effect is the same as it was for Paul, but the sole cause is now said to be the working of the Spirit.

The Greek Fathers agree with Paul that the transformation of believers is due to the death and resurrection of Jesus, but for them it takes place with the Kingdom of God in view, and not, as for him, in the Kingdom already present. According to their teaching, believers live no longer in the world, but in the intermediate realm of the Spirit, until the Kingdom comes. Ignatius and Justin set the seal of martyrdom on this doctrine—noble of its kind—of world-renunciation through the Spirit.

. . . .

Western theology is mainly concerned with the doctrine of the forgiveness of sins, and its task is to interpret the death of Jesus in such a way that men may find in it forgiveness ever available, ever renewed, for all the lapses of which they become guilty. Only thus can believers have the assurance that their redemption has already been achieved; for them the Kingdom is not at hand, but far away, and the whole of their life in this world has to be lived in the midst of temptation.

Neither Jesus himself nor Paul offers this view of the efficacy of the atoning death on the Cross.

Jesus takes it for granted, in his preaching, that God in his tender mercy guarantees forgiveness to those who truly repent. The Lord's Prayer attaches the condition that the petitioner must have forgiven all his debtors.

Two sayings of Jesus, from the later period of his activity, give an atoning significance to his death:

The Son of man came not to be ministered unto, but to minister, and to give his life a ransom for many. *Mark x.* 45.

This is my blood of the covenant, which is shed for many. *Mark xiv.* 24. (. . . unto remission of sins. *Matthew xxvi,* 28.)

The atoning value of his death, according to Jesus, does not interfere with the direct flowing of forgiveness from the tender mercy of God, but adds something to it. Its object, as he sees it, is not to enable God to forgive, but to save the faithful from having to pay the penalty of their sins in the tribulation preceding the advent of the Messiah, to put an end to the power of the evil one without exposing them to his final onslaught, and bring in the Kingdom of God without this ghastly prelude.

Jesus undertakes his Passion in order that the last petition of the Lord's prayer may be fulfilled: "Lead us not into temptation, but deliver us from evil." "Temptation" means "trial," and refers to the pre-Messianic tribulation which was to take place before the coming of the Kingdom, according to late Jewish eschatology. The words and deeds of Jesus can only be understood when due attention is paid to his pre-occupation with this dreadful anticipation.

No teaching about the atonement is given by Jesus to his disciples; he demands of them no theory about it, no faith in it. It remains his secret. He neither poses as the coming Messiah nor seeks for faith in himself as such. It is enough that his followers believe in the coming of the Kingdom of God, and prepare for entrance into it by repentance and fulfilment of his higher moral law. Who he is, and what he has done for them will come home to them when the Kingdom is there, and they have entered into it without passing through the great tribulation.

The meaning of the Passion for Jesus himself is rooted in eschatology, its object being to destroy the force of a certain prediction. The many, who are to be ransomed, are believers who await with him the coming of the Kingdom, not mankind as a whole. His own generation is the last. The end of this world is close at hand.

We cannot tell how far the disciples and the first Christians were concerned with the problem of the pre-Messianic tribulation, or how far they were persuaded that for them atonement, having been wrought by the death of Jesus, would not involve this tribulation. After the crucifixion they found themselves in a situation which left no room for that way of thinking. They knew, from the hints which he had given them, that he was the Messiah and Son of Man, about to be revealed in his glory, and that his death effected an atonement, involving their own forgiveness, and the coming of the Kingdom.

Having no precise doctrine of the atonement, the apostles and first believers took the simple view that through his death Jesus had gained the forgiveness of sins for them, and so they would escape condemnation in the judgment which would take place at the coming of the Kingdom of God. Thus the atoning death of Jesus was given a new meaning at the very beginning; the original idea of Jesus himself was displaced by the view that it was actually the necessary condition of the divine forgiveness of sins. This created an insoluble problem. How is it conceivable that God only forgives sins on the ground that Jesus has died? How is such a view to be reconciled with the fact that in the Lord's

Prayer Jesus teaches us to ask for forgiveness as if it could only be granted through the mercy of God to those who forgive their debtors?

It was centuries before anybody had the courage to face this problem. The first really to do so was the schoolman, Anselm of Canterbury (1033–1109), in his famous writing, *Cur Deus homo* (Why must God become man?). He argues that God's honour has been damaged by man's sin, and that there can be no forgiveness without satisfaction. This cannot be provided by sinful man. But in his love God means to forgive. Only a human being who is at the same time God, and therefore perfect and sinless, can give adequate satisfaction. Therefore Jesus came into the world, and achieved this through his voluntary death, thus enabling God to act both with justice and with love. All subsequent efforts to solve the problem follow in the track of this completely unsatisfactory explanation.

Those who cannot reconcile their conception of God with a belief that he needs a sacrifice before he can forgive sins are at liberty to look simply to his mercy for forgiveness, and to find redemption in the gift of the Spirit of God through Jesus, whereby we are taken out of this world and brought to God.

. . . .

The fundamental meaning of the death of Jesus for Paul is that he has thereby brought to an end the dominion of the powers of evil in the world, and set in motion the process, shown in his resurrection, of transforming the natural world into the supernatural. This is in full harmony with the view held by Jesus himself of the effect of his self-sacrifice in death.

Paul is giving expression to the simple early Christian belief in the forgiveness of sins, when he says that God overlooks the sins committed formerly on the ground of the atonement wrought by Jesus (Rom. iii, 25), not reckoning them (II Cor. v, 19), and that Jesus delivers believers from the wrath to come (I Thess. i, 10; Rom. v, 9).

But he does not hold to the early view that the death of Jesus makes it possible for the Kingdom to come, and by its atoning efficacy procures forgiveness for believers on the Day of Judgment. His position is that believers are already free from all sins, basing this on his theory that the transformation of the natural world into the supernatural has already begun and is going on in those who die and rise again with Christ. "We are dead to sin." "He that hath died is justified from sin." "Ye are not in the flesh, but in the spirit." (Rom. vi, 2, 7; viii, 9). Sin no longer comes into consideration for believers who have, with Paul, the assurance that they are sharers in a real and complete forgiveness of sins.

His polemic against those Christians who are still under the sway of the Jewish view that righteousness is earned by practising circumcision and observing the Law leads Paul to fashion the doctrine of justification by faith in Jesus Christ alone. "But now apart from the Law a righteousness of God hath been manifested, . . . even the righteousness of God through faith in Jesus Christ; . . . justified freely by his grace through the redemption that is in Christ Jesus" (Rom. iii, 21–24).

This assurance of already possessing the full reality of redemption, which goes so far beyond the experience of the first Christians, rested for Paul on his conviction that believers are already risen again, since union with Jesus, through faith and the power of his death, involves dying and rising again with him; they are already in the Kingdom of God. The righteousness which is the qualification for entrance into the Kingdom is no longer something to be striven after. Believers must have it already through their faith in Jesus; otherwise they could not find themselves sharing in the resurrection, which proves that they are already partakers in the Kingdom of God.

Paul's doctrine is not one of continuous forgiveness, but of full forgiveness. He does not take into consideration the possibility of going on sinning after becoming a believer. But his view of justification by faith alone is of fundamental importance for the later rise and development of the doctrine of continuous forgiveness. This made its appearance when Paul's doctrine was separated from eschatology and from the eschatological mysticism of union with Christ in his death and resurrection.

. . . .

Early Christianity did not contemplate the possibility that further generations of men would make their appearance upon the earth after the death of Jesus. But that is what happened. So it became necessary to widen the scope of the doctrine of the atonement, in order to make it possible for men, yet to be born, to obtain the forgiveness of sins on becoming believers.

If forgiveness becomes available for men of all ages, it must be thought of as being continuous. That was not necessary at the beginning, when the Kingdom was expected immediately. What men needed then was the forgiveness of sins committed before their conversion. The early Christians' view was that this was procured by the death of Jesus and became theirs in baptism. The presumption was that they would continue sinless during the short period of waiting for the Kingdom. Forgiveness takes place, for them as for Paul, only once (cf. Rom. iii. 25). But those who have to live the whole of their life in the natural sinful world need to be assured that believers go on being forgiven again and again for the lapses of which they are guilty in the course of time.

There was, however, a great difficulty in the way of the development of the new doctrine. Baptism could only mean what it had meant from the beginning, *viz.*, the bestowal of forgiveness for past sins. Its character could not be altered, and it remained unaffected by the abandonment of an immediate expectation of the coming of the Kingdom. The problem thus arose as to whether post-baptismal sins can be forgiven at all, and if they can, by what means this is to be accomplished.

At first the possibility was strongly denied. The author of the epistle to the Hebrews, writing between the years 70 and 80, says that "as touching those who were once enlightened . . . and were made partakers of the Holy Spirit, and tasted the good word of God, and the powers of the age to come, and then fell away, it is impossible to renew them again unto repentance, seeing they crucify to themselves the Son of God afresh, and put him to an open shame" (Hebr. vi. 4–6).

Hermas, a Roman layman, at the beginning of the second century, asserts the possibility of obtaining forgiveness for later sins by means of a second repentance, in addition to that which led to baptism. He does this on the strength of a revelation brought to him by an "Angel of repentance" who appeared to him in the form of a shepherd. In his book, *The*

Shepherd of Hermas, which appeared about A.D. 130, he announces that God in his mercy is willing to give believers the possibility of regaining their standing in grace by means of a repeated repentance. The Church could do no other than accept this view, which allowed her to take back sinners whom she had been compelled to excommunicate, after they had renewed their repentance.

But the atoning death of Jesus only happened once; and the same is true of the forgiveness which he procured. The recognition of a forgiveness for sins committed after baptism places the Church in the peculiar position of having to admit that besides the forgiveness made possible by the death of Jesus there is another, not resting on that foundation, but granted directly through God's mercy to those who, by repentance and other good works, are found worthy of this grace. Among good works recognised, in addition to public repentance, as having satisfaction-value are—suffering, which has atoning virtue, faithfulness under persecution, deeds of love, and the conversion of heretics.

The Church is the stewardess of this supplementary forgiveness. She prescribes what the sinner must do in the way of repentance and satisfaction, exercises over-sight, and makes sure how far he has done his duty. When she judges that he can have found forgiveness with God, she takes him back into the congregation. She makes no claim to forgive, but feels herself to be the announcer of the forgiveness which God has granted.

But the matter cannot rest there, with the permission of only one supplementary forgiveness; it gradually comes to repentance procuring forgiveness again and again. And then there is the problem of differentiating between venial sins and those which are too serious to be forgiven. Thus in the course of time the idea of continuous forgiveness was reached.

Augustine (354–430) lays it down as a principle that forgiveness is available within the Church for all sins committed after baptism, provided appropriate satisfaction is made. Outside the Church there is no pardon. Not to believe in the continuous forgiveness of sins within the Church is to commit the sin against the Holy Spirit.

Contemporary new ideas mentioned by Augustine in connexion with continuous forgiveness are that of Purgatory and that of the offering of prayer, alms and the Sacrifice of the Mass by the living on behalf of the dead, that they may find forgiveness.

Purgatory is not punishment in hell, but only a possibility, held out to the sinner after death, of completing, by the endurance of torment, the repentance of which he fell short in his earthly life.

The idea that in the Mass the body and blood of Jesus are offered up afresh as an atoning sacrifice to God appears first in Cyprian, bishop of Carthage, who died as a martyr in 258. Augustine understands this in a purely spiritual sense. The realistic view established itself under Pope Gregory I (590–604), *viz.*, that in the Mass Jesus is offered as a sacrifice sacramentally again and again, to bring the benefit of the atonement to the living and the dead. This sacramental repetition implies that the forgiveness brought about by Jesus on Golgotha avails, not only for sins committed before baptism, but also—as it were by a side-channel—for those committed after. By letting its priests carry out this repetition of the atoning sacrifice of Jesus, the Church helps to establish the view that it brings about and bestows the forgiveness of sins, instead of merely announcing it as something which God does when adequate satisfaction is offered.

Subsequently it became customary for more and more Masses to be celebrated. These were no longer congregational acts of worship, but were only intended to convey the atoning power of the sacramental repetition of the death of Jesus to those, living or dead, on whose behalf they were held. Towards the end of the Middle Ages all Churches had, in addition to the high altar, side-altars at which these special Masses were said.

Continuous forgiveness became generally easier and easier to obtain during the Middle Ages—and more and more dependent upon outward performances. It gradually became the custom to secure exemption from the penance ordered by the priests on the ground of merits or of payments to the Church. Those who took part in the Crusades obtained full exemption. From the twelfth century, those who did not go to war against the infidel could get their indulgence by the payment of money. The Schoolmen justified the dispensation of indulgences by the Popes on the ground that they were the custodians of the accumulated merits of the saints. In the year 1477 Pope Sixtus IV (1471–1484) announced that indulgences were also valid for souls in Purgatory, and would shorten the time of their purification.

It was widely felt at the end of the Middle Ages that this state of affairs was unsatisfactory. But it would not meet the case, simply to reform the doctrine of continuous forgiveness and return to the purity of its original formulation.

Then there appeared on the scene, in Martin Luther (1483–1546), a man of outstanding religious personality, who

103

first objected to the unspiritual practices which had come to be associated with the Church's doctrine of continuous forgiveness, and then proceeded to question its underlying principle.

. . . .

As a monk, Luther tried to reach the assurance of forgiveness along the orthodox lines. He did not succeed. In his agony, he asked himself whether he was not one of those predestined to damnation, since all his penance, and the absolution which he received, failed to bring him the deliverance for which he looked.

Through Augustine he was led to Paul, whose doctrine of justification by faith alone, without works, was the light which penetrated his darkness. His final spiritual deliverance took place in 1512, and he owed it to Paul. We have the working out of his new conception of continuous forgiveness on the ground of faith in the operation of the atoning death of Jesus, in his lectures at the University of Wittenberg on the Psalms (1513–1515), Romans (1515–1516), Galatians (1516) and Hebrews (1517).

Luther inevitably discovered that the Catholic view of baptism was the basis of the doctrine of continuous forgiveness as dependent on justification by works and not by faith. It was this which ruled out the attribution of continuous forgiveness to the atoning death of Jesus. It was responsible for the view that post-baptismal sins required justification by works to obtain forgiveness.

But the effect of baptism should not be confined to the forgiveness of past sins through Jesus' death; it ought to secure for the believer the possibility of finding continuous forgiveness at the Cross. So Luther propounded the doctrine that baptism "is the beginning and gateway of all grace and forgiveness." The pardon which men need every day is just the renewal of baptismal grace, freely given by God on the ground of faith in the atoning work of Christ.

The conflict between Luther and the Catholic Church turned finally upon the doctrine of baptism. Historically Luther was in the wrong. He intended to restore the simple original doctrine, from which he thought the Church had departed. But it was the Church, and not Luther, that held the old idea of baptism. Religiously, however, his view was right, for it made it possible to believe in the continuous forgiveness of sins as coming directly from God through Christ.

The Catholic doctrine of baptism is the only thing which has been preserved unaltered throughout the centuries from the first age of eschatological faith. It was a big step in the movement away from eschatology when Luther formulated his doctrine of baptism without any reference to the last things.

Luther's doctrine of forgiveness is not identical with Paul's; it is a re-statement of it without the primitive eschatology. It was because Paul was the only great thinker in the early Church who saw clearly that redemption, like the Kingdom, was not something in the future, but a present reality, that Luther found in him the substance and the spirit of his own doctrine of salvation now through the continuous forgiveness of sins. The latter meant for him what the nearness of the Kingdom meant for Paul.

So Luther sounds the same note of victory as Paul, a note which had not been heard in Christian preaching since Paul's day. His sense of triumph leads him away from that denial of the world to which the Church was still committed in spite of its weakened eschatology. He does not ask for renunciation of the world as the expression of true Christianity; what he enjoins is faithful performance of daily duties in the way of our earthly calling and the practice of love to our neighbour. He erects an ideal of Christian perfection which attaches real value to the state, to marriage, and to lawful occupations, and views daily labour, however humble, as service required by God. He feels himself moved to agree with the affirmation of life and the world, although he does not break away from that pessimistic judgment of the world which is involved in the later form of eschatology. In this he was prophetic of what was to happen later in the history of Protestantism.

Luther also combines the conservative with the progressive in that he attaches great importance to the acknowledgment that his doctrine agrees with that of the Church of the first centuries, and yet does not make this agreement a rallying point for Protestants, but summons them to study the Gospel in the New Testament, recognising it as their supreme and sole authority.

This principle is the inspiration of free and dauntless search for religious truth. Luther could not measure the scope of this study of the original Gospel and the recognition of its supreme authority; the road, which he opened up, led further afield than he could ever have imagined. And yet, by following this road, Protestantism completed what Luther had begun. His rejection of the Catholic doctrine of continuous forgiveness as based on primitive Christian baptism, in favour of a new one, constitutes the penultimate stage in the movement of Christianity away from eschatology. The last stage is the surrender of the eschatological idea of the

Kingdom of God, with the acceptance of a view that is not determined by its relation to the last things. This is the experience destined for Protestantism in its effort to get back to the true Gospel.

. . . .

What then, is being done to effect this surrender and eliminate eschatology from the conception of the Kingdom? How are matters going?

The fundamental pre-supposition necessary for this change is provided by the existence of a new attitude towards the world. The affirmation and acceptance of the world begin to take their place beside the traditional Christian denial and rejection of it, which resulted from eschatology.

When it first makes its appearance in the fourteenth century, the positive attitude can hardly be described as a philosophy; it consists rather in the rejection of the spirit of the Middle Ages and all that it comprises.

With the contemporary rise and growth of natural science, a more profound level is reached. The order and harmony of the universe come into view as the result of the astronomy of a Copernicus (1473–1543), a Kepler (1571–1630) and a Galileo (1564–1642). Advances in knowledge and skill encourage a belief in progress, and this adds to the strength and vitality of the acceptance of life and the world. The spirit of man acquires an unprecedented confidence in human capacity and creative power in every field. Thus by the time of a Giordano Bruno (1548–1600) the new attitude has attained to the stature of a philosophy.

Clarified and deepened under the influence of the achievements of natural science, the movement then gains strength by appropriating the ethics of later Stoicism, as found in the writings of Cicero (106–43 B.C.) and developed by Seneca (4 B.C.–A.D. 65), Epictetus (b. about A.D. 50) and Marcus Aurelius (120–180). Hugo Grotius (1583–1645) shews how completely the modern acceptance of life and the world is under the influence of the Stoic ideal of humanity. Here is something absolutely new in the intellectual history of Europe: a philosophical acceptance of the world with a moral outlook. Herein lies the differentia of modern European man, as compared with man in earlier times. He has a new intellectual attitude, believing in progress, determined to do all he can to help the world onward and upward, and disposed to universal charity.

The ethical quality of the new outlook makes it acceptable to Christians, who are prepared for it by the ethical teaching of Jesus. For although the latter adopted a negative attitude to life and the world, it did not lose itself in absolute pessimism. That would have involved accepting the ideal of inactivity, whereas Christianity means active love.

The reason why the ethic of Jesus is practical is to be found in the fact that the eschatological denial of the world does not go as far as the Indian. It does nor reject existence as such in favour of non-existence, like the Indian, but only the natural, imperfect, painful world in prospect of the world of the Kingdom of God. Its view is that man must prove and demonstrate his calling to take part in the perfecting of existence by living an active moral life in the natural world. The ethic of Jesus has an affinity with the ethical philosophy of world-acceptance in so far as its ideal is one of activity.

Modern Protestant Christianity takes a long time to break away from world-denial. The hymns of the Church remain under its influence until late in the eighteenth century. Escape from the world provides the leading motif in the cantatas of Johann Sebastian Bach (1685–1750); yet the Protestantism of that time is moving irresistibly in the direction of a philosophy of world-acceptance. It is not conscious of the step that it is taking; the passage from the old to the new is concealed by the fact that there is so much in common between Christianity and ethical world-acceptance. The point of contact is in the ethic: the Stoic ideal of humanity comes very close to Jesus' ideal of love. So the passage of Christianity in the new age from the ethical negative to the ethical positive view takes place without observation and without conflict.

Belief in the Kingdom of God now takes a new lease of life. It no longer looks for its coming, self-determined, as an eschatological cosmic event, but regards it as something ethical and spiritual, not bound up with the last things, but to be realised with the co-operation of men.

In ancient and mediaeval times, Christians had no faith in progress, no urge to go forward, no idea that things could be moving onward and upward; yet it never occurred to them that they were in an unnatural situation so long as their religious life was based on the idea that the Kingdom of God lay far away in the future. It seemed obvious to them that passivity concerning the Kingdom was the only possible attitude.

It is otherwise with those of the new age who are under the influence of the ethical affirmation of the world. What they think is that the Kingdom is something ethical and religious, to be conceived as developing in this world, and requiring ethical effort on the part of believers. This is so obvious to them that they can conceive of no other way of looking at the subject; they understand the Gospels to say that Jesus came into this world to found the Kingdom, and to call men into it as fellow-workers. Just as Luther substituted his non-eschatological view of baptism for that of the early Church, convinced that it was the authentic teaching of the Gospels, so modern Protestantism substitutes its view of the Kingdom of God and its coming for the eschatological view which Jesus presented as if it really represented the original. Historically both are wrong; but religiously both are right.

Only as it comes to be understood as something ethical and spiritual, rather than supernatural, as something to be realised rather than expected, can the Kingdom of God regain, in our faith, the force that it had for Jesus and the early Church. Christianity must have a firm hold of this, if it is to remain true to itself, as it was at the beginning,—religion dominated by the idea of the Kingdom of God. What the Kingdom of God is in reality is shown by the part which it plays in the life of faith. The precise conception which is held of its coming is a matter of secondary consideration. In spite of many fundamental differences from the past, modern Protestant Christianity remains true to the Gospel since it is still the religion of a living faith in the Kingdom of God.

. . . .

About the end of the eighteenth and the beginning of the nineteenth century, "Lives of Jesus" began to appear, these being the first efforts to reach a historical understanding of his earthly life and teaching. Mention may be made of the works of Johann Jakob Hess (1768–1772)—in three volumes

110

—Franz Volkmar Reinhard (1781), Johann Gottfried Herder (1796), Heinrich Eberhard Gottleib Paulus (1828) and Karl August Hase (1829).

According to these, Jesus appeared before the Jews, whose hopes of the Kingdom of God and the Messiah were materialistic and mundane, as the true Messiah, quite different in character, who made the beginning of a Kingdom of God which meant the control of human life by the Spirit of God. The idea that Jesus spiritualised the Jewish hope of the Kingdom continued to dominate historical and critical theology during the second half of the nineteenth century. It was set forth by Adolf Harnack in his famous lectures at Berlin University in the winter of 1899–1900 under the title, *Das Wesen des Christentums* (What is Christianity?).

Even at that time there were grounds for questioning this idea. More careful study of the documents of later Jewish eschatology revealed the fact that their fundamental conceptions were shared by sayings of Jesus concerning the Kingdom of God and the Messiah. This is specially clear in the records of Matthew and Mark, which in this respect are shown to be the oldest. But it seemed impossible to believe that Jesus should not have held views about the Kingdom of God and his own Messianic calling that were in harmony with the inwardness and depth of his ideal of love.

At the beginning of this century, therefore, the difficulty was overcome by putting forward the theory that the sayings in question were not actually uttered by Jesus. They had been introduced into the tradition by the early Church, which was still under the influence of the later Jewish eschatology. Harnack and others even suggested that Jesus was able to combine elements of that eschatology with his

111

own spiritual view of the Kingdom in some way that is beyond our comprehension.

But already in 1892 Johannes Weiss, of Heidelberg, had shown that it is impossible to differentiate the eschatological view of the Kingdom and the Messiah, held by Jesus, from that of later Judaism—in his study, *Die Predigt Jesu von Reiche Gottes* (The Preaching of Jesus concerning the Kingdom of God), based on Matthew and Mark. I carried Johannes Weiss's argument to its conclusion in my sketch of the life of Jesus, *Das Messianitäts- und Leidensgeheimnis* (1901) and my *Geschichte der Leben-Jesu-Forschung* (1906), showing that eschatology not only coloured the thoughts of Jesus, but also determined his actions.

Those who have the courage to let Matthew and Luke mean what they say must agree that Jesus shared the later Jewish view of the advent of the Kingdom of God, not spiritualising it, but using it as a vehicle for his profound and powerful ideal of love.

It is hard for us to bring ourselves to the point of admitting that Jesus, who is uniquely endowed with the Spirit of God, and is for us the supreme revealer of religious and spiritual truth, does not stand above his age in the way that might seem to be demanded by the significance which he has for all ages.

What we should prefer is that we, and men of every age, might find in Jesus the final truth of religion available in a form that need never be changed. And now we are confronted by the fact that he shared the outlook of an age long past, which is to us mistaken and unacceptable. Why should Christianity have to endure this? Is it not a wound for which there is no balm? Ought we not to maintain the

112

absolute inerrancy of Jesus in matters of religion? Are we not rejecting his authority?

Both Johannes Weiss and I have suffered severely through the compulsion which truth laid upon us to put forward something which was bound to offend Christian faith.

To me, however, Jesus remains what he was. Not for a single moment have I had to struggle for my conviction that in him is the supreme spiritual and religious authority, though his expectation of the speedy advent of a supernatural Kingdom of God was not fulfilled, and we cannot make it our own.

The difficulty can only be overcome by a right apprehension of what is meant by the inerrancy of Jesus.

Our assumption of the limitation of his knowledge does not mean that he had an understanding of nature equal to that attained, or ever attainable, by modern science, but refrained from using it. The historical Jesus stands before us as one who shared naturally the outlook of his time. This is not a pose, but an actual reality. Anything else would involve a dissimulation which we can never associate with him.

If Jesus thinks like his contemporaries about the world and what happens in it, then his view of the coming of the Kingdom of God must resemble that of later Judaism.

It is perfectly clear to anyone who studies deeply the way in which progress is achieved in history that what is absolutely new does not easily establish itself, and if, for any reason, it does succeed, it is apt to appear unnatural and questionable. So we must believe that, if Jesus had appeared with a fully spiritualised view of the Kingdom and its coming, his proclamation of it would never have been believed. The ancient world, Jewish, Greek and Roman, would have had no point of contact with such an announcement. To enable it to do its work naturally, every new idea must be in some way embedded in what is old, and thus be linked with that which preceded it. Jesus ends a series of parables of the Kingdom of God with the remarkable saying, "Therefore every scribe who hath been made a disciple to the Kingdom of heaven is like unto a man that is a householder, which bringeth forth out of his treasure things new and old" (Matt. xiii. 52).

Truth cannot dissociate itself from the time process; it must work within it. Jesus spiritualises the conception of the Kingdom of God, in that he brings it into subjection to his ideal and ethic of love. In due time this transforms the conception of the Kingdom.

Spiritual truth is concerned with the knowledge of what we must become spiritually in order to be in a right relationship to God. It is complete in itself. It is intuitive knowledge of what ought to be in the realm of the spirit. All other knowledge is of a different kind, having to do, not with what happens in us, but with what goes on in the world,— a field in which understanding can only be limited and liable to change.

The conception of the realisation of a spiritual idea on a universal scale is conditioned by the conception of the world and its events which prevails at a particular time. The fact that Jesus thinks of the realisation of the Kingdom of God in a way that is not justified by events does not call in question his authority as a unique revealer of spiritual truth; it only challenges the traditional view of his personality and authority. Christian faith, under the influence of Greek metaphysics, was pleased to confer upon him a divinity and a divine inerrancy to which he made no claim. We shall only deal successfully with the problem of his unfulfilled promise when we turn back to see exactly how he confronts us in the two oldest Gospels. He is so great, that the discovery that he belongs to his age can do him no harm. He remains our spiritual Lord.

All attempts to avoid the admission that Jesus held a view of the Kingdom of God and its coming which was not fulfilled and cannot be adopted by us involve the shirking of the truth. Devotion to truth in this matter is of the essence of spiritual life. Faith which refuses to face indisputable facts is but little faith. Truth is always gain, however hard it is to accommodate ourselves to it. To linger in any kind of untruth proves to be a departure from the straight way of faith.

. . . .

The modern view of the Kingdom of God and its coming creates a spiritual situation comparable with that of Jesus and his little flock and of the early Church. Again, after many centuries, the Kingdom of God has become a live question. Again mankind as a whole is changing its mind as to what it really means.

Modern faith finds the beginning of the Kingdom of God in Jesus and in the Spirit which came into the world with him. We no longer leave the fate of mankind to be decided at the end of the world. The time in which we live summons us to new faith in the Kingdom of God.

We are no longer content, like the generations before us, to believe in the Kingdom that comes of itself at the end of time. Mankind to-day must either realise the Kingdom of

God or perish. The very tragedy of our present situation compels us to devote ourselves in faith to its realisation.

We are at the beginning of the end of the human race. The question before it is whether it will use for beneficial purposes or for purposes of destruction the power which modern science has placed in its hands. So long as its capacity for destruction was limited, it was possible to hope that reason would set a limit to disaster. Such an illusion is impossible to-day, when its power is illimitable. Our only hope is that the Spirit of God will strive with the spirit of the world and will prevail.

The last petition of the Lord's Prayer has again its original meaning for us as a prayer for deliverance from the dominion of the evil powers of the world. These are no less real to us as working in men's minds, instead of being embodied in angelic beings opposed to God. The first believers set their hope solely upon the Kingdom of God in expectation of the end of the world; we do it in expectation of the end of the human race.

The Spirit shows us the signs of the time and their meaning.

Belief in the Kingdom of God makes the biggest demands of all the articles of the Christian faith. It means believing the seemingly impossible,—the conquest of the spirit of the world by the Spirit of God. We look with confidence for the miracle to be wrought through the Spirit.

The miracle must happen in us before it can happen in the world. We dare not set our hope on our own efforts to create the conditions of God's Kingdom in the world. We must indeed labour for its realisation. But there can be no Kingdom of God in the world without the Kingdom of God in our hearts. The starting-point is our determined effort to bring every thought and action under the sway of the Kingdom of God. Nothing can be achieved without inwardness. The Spirit of God will only strive against the spirit of the world when it has won its victory over that spirit in our hearts.